SABRINA FISHER REECE

Small Business Basics

How to sustain a small business in todays market

In59Seconds Publishing Co

First edition

I dedicate this book to every person who ever worked for Braids By SaBrina, A New Vision Dreadlock Studio, Just-In Time Barber Shop, or Inked 4 Life Tattoo Studio. Thank you for trusting me to provide a stable place of income. I love all of you. Thank you for growing and learning with me. I wish you all an abundance of success. Remember, "All Things Are Possible," so never stop creating a beautiful life for yourselves. I pray from me, you learned hope, dedication, and resilience.

–SaBrina

Contents

1

Your Entrepreneurial Blueprint: Steps to Start Today

Start where you are. Use what you have. Do what you can."
-Arthur Ashe

🔥 YOUR STARTUP BLUEPRINT (Read This First)

1. Pick Your Business Name
Make it clear, memorable, and meaningful
Search online to ensure it's available
Choose something easy to spell and easy to say
2. Register Your Business
File a DBA or LLC
Get your EIN

Secure your business license
3. Set Up Your Brand
Create a simple logo (Canva is free)
Pick 2–3 brand colors and stick to them.
Define your message: What do you offer? Who do you serve?

4. Create Your First Marketing Tools
Business cards
Flyers/postcards
Instagram business page
Facebook business page
Google My Business listing
Basic website or booking link (Wix, Square, Linktree)

5. Start Telling People About Your Business
Share your story
Post consistently
Network locally
Hand out flyers
Be visible everywhere

6. Be Consistent, Even When You're Scared
Set weekly goals
Market daily
Stay disciplined even when it's slow

7. Start Today — Not Tomorrow
You don't need perfect.
You don't need permission.
You just need to make the decision to begin.

Now the Chapter Begins...

There is an entrepreneur inside every single one of us. Some people grow up dreaming of owning a business — I wasn't one of them. Not even close. I never imagined myself as a business owner. I didn't have a five-year plan. I didn't have a mentor. I didn't have a blueprint.

What I *did* have was a desperate need to survive.

At twenty years old, I went through my first divorce. Suddenly, I was alone. No mother — she wasn't there. No father — he wasn't there either. My grandmother, the only real mother I had ever known, had been murdered in front of me when I was 17 years old and I was far from healed from that. I had a small son and baby daughter depending on me to figure out life immediately.

No safety net.

No backup plan.

No emotional support.

No money.

Just me - a hurting young woman who could braid hair and refused to give up.

But this is where your entrepreneurial journey begins. Right here with what you have even before you feel ready. START! Design your business in your mind and START!

The odds were definitely against me, and that why I want you to know that You Can Do This Too. I do not possess any secret powers that God didn't also give you. Yes my motivation may initially have been survival but at some point in the business journey I tapped into a magnificent energy that we all have. I call it **"The Inspiration for Creation"**. There is a creator in us all. You simply have to sit down and make concrete decisions on exactly why type of business you want. Yes it helps is it is something you do naturally and are passionate about it.

Here's the truth most people never say:

20% of small businesses fail in the first year and 50% fail by year five. Your job is to make sure your business does not fail. I never once entertained the idea of failure for Braids By SaBrina. I had no idea it would turn into the largest and most famous braiding salon in Los Angeles, but I'm sure grateful it did.

Systematically design your business. Start in your mind first. Every idea begins in the mind, so sit down, take a deep breath and visualize every precise detail, exactly how you want it. That truly is the first step. There is not one business that exists, that did not start as a idea in the mind of the owner.

Only about 1/3rd make it ten years

But numbers never scared me and do not let them scare you.

4

Numbers didn't raise me, life did. Numbers didn't make me, survival did. Numbers didn't keep me going, purpose did.

If someone like me - a young Black girl from Compton, with all kinds of trauma abandoned by her mother, grieving the loss of her beloved Grandmother, recently divorced, raising two young children-could create a long-standing brand with nearly 1,700 braiders over three decades... then you can build yours too. All things are possible and do not allow anyone to tell you any different.

You will have to believe in your business and not expect others to. It's your vision not theirs. So do not set yourself up for failure, or get your feelings hurt by expecting family and friends to comprehend and *SEE* your vision. This is a gift God gave to you, you do not need cheerleaders. I was and have always been my biggest cheerleader.

Step 1: Choose Your Business Name

Before anything else - before you design, post, print, or promote - choose your name. Be certain and don't flip flop back and forth with the name. My business names were **"Braids By SaBrina"**, **"Inked 4 Life Tattoo Studio"**, **"Braids By SaBrina Braiding School"**, **"Just-In-Time Barber Shop"**, **"A New Vision Dreadlock Studio"**, and **"A New Vision Sound Meditation Studio"**, and **"In59Seconds Publishing Co."**

A name holds power and a name creates identity. A name is the first brick in your foundation. Get clear on the name because there are so many more bricks to lay.

Braids By SaBrina was simple, memorable, and meaningful. And yours should be too. I monopolized the market and flooded the city with that name. You can still google it today and find an enormous amount of content online. But understand, I started

5

my business when the internet did not exist. I walked street by street and put flyers in each mailbox while pushing a baby in a stroller with my first daughter Joi in it.

Make sure your name is:
Easy to spell
Easy to remember
Easy to pronounce
Not Common
Clearly connected to what you do
Then search it online to make sure no one else has it. Register it at your cities registrar department. Then go to Go Daddy.com and purchase the URL. Those actions sets you apart from others who are still contemplating and it plants your feet solidly in the business world.

Step 2: Register, License, and Become Real
Do not skip this part.
A business becomes official when you:
Get your EIN
File your DBA or LLC
Get your business license (Professional Occupations & Commercial)
Separate business and personal finances
This protects you legally and elevates you professionally.
I didn't have anyone to teach me any of this.
But YOU have me now - and I'm giving you the blueprint I never had.

Step 3: Build Your First Marketing Tools
I started in my home in 1989 and opened the brick and mortar

in 1996, **there was no My Space, Facebook, Instagram, no TikTok, no Google, no Canva, no YouTube tutorials.**
There was only:
A kitchen table
Neon poster boards from Thrifty's
Thick markers
A roll of tape
A staple gun and some cable ties, and my commitment to be successful.

I hand-wrote every sign: "**Braids By SaBrina"** I walked through Compton, Watts, Inglewood, Gardena and South Central, putting flyers on cars and in mailboxes, putting up signs with cable ties on bus stops, light poles, chain linked fences, anywhere someone might see them. And guess what? Those signs built my first clientele. They not only brought in my first customers, they walked in the first Braiders I hired. I circulated a paper flyer in the neighborhood near the salon saying 'Braid Shop Coming Soon" a month before the doors opened. So on opening day I had five braiders and a customer in every chair.

Today, YOU have multiple choices to advertise:
Etsy
Instagram
TikTok
Canva
Facebook
Twitter
QR codes
Google My Business
Online booking sites

Digital business cards
Reels
Short-form video marketing

The entire world fits in your hand. If I built my business with poster boards and tape...imagine what YOU can build with everything you have today. There are NO Limitations accept those you accept in your own mind.

Step 4: Be Consistent - Even When You're Scared

Consistency is more powerful than talent it is more powerful than money. More powerful than confidence. I posted every weekend and weekdays when I was not working. I braided until my fingers hurt. I worked until neighbors complained to my landlord that I was running a business out of my $500 a month apartment on 109th and Normandie.

Eventually I hired my first Braider in my home. Her name was Niecy. I quickly outgrew my home business I found a space on 65th & Normandie. It wasn't fancy. It wasn't pretty. I had folding chair and tables from target. It took a few months before I could afford to buy used styling chairs, but not one client complained.

When I did get the styling chair I got them from a salon whole seller called "Olsens" that had a huge wear house on Western Ave filled with used salon furniture. Do not, I repeat Do Not go out a buy brand new expensive furniture for your business. If you are good at what you do , no one will care or even notice the used furniture.

My first salon wasn't perfect. But it was all mine. I didn't beg, borrow or steal to get it. I worked my but off. Going home some evenings with swollen wrist and ankles....but it was worth it. the beginning of the **BRAIDS BY SABRINA** legacy.

No loans.
  No investors.
  No business degree.
  Just determination
  Just courage.
  Just hustle.
  Just faith.

Step 5: Start Today — Start Small — Start Scared

Your entrepreneurial blueprint doesn't require millions. Do not go into debt and do not take out loans. Keep your day job while you are building your small business. Each pay check purchase something you need for your new business. Keep everything logged and itemized.

Building a successful small business requires movement. Do something towards the advancement of your business every day. Use what you have access to. Use the free advertising services of the internet.

Learn as you go. I started with nothing – but I STARTED. Do not make excuses or wait for anyone to help you. It is your Small business, your baby. Do not depend on others. I can not stress that enough. You are truly stronger than you think.

You may not have support and you may not have a lot of money. You may not feel ready. You may be afraid to fail but readiness is not a requirement. Willingness is. You're reading this because something in your spirit knows you were made for more. So let me say this again:

Start today-Start small-Start scared-Just start.

Everything you dream of lives on the other side of that first step.

Omg! I just found pictures online of my Original Braids by SaBrina Signs from 1989..Wow..I used to paint these myself with waterpaint..This Is How It All Began!

The very first Braid By SaBrina signs.

First Braids By SaBrina Staff

After the Rodney King riots in the city of Los Angeles, there were alot of businesses destroyed, which let a lot of vacant lots. Those lots are were I hung the very first Braids By SaBrina signs. Initially I painted them with flouresant water paint. I kept it simple, huge letters and my phone number.

my very first story front on 65th and Normandie in 1996

SaBrina and the Braids by SaBrina Staff in 1998

Barber Shop I opened for my son Justin

Braids By SaBrina Christmas Staff picture

Article written about SaBrina in the SCOOP News paper

2

Trial and Error-Learning as You Grow

"Wisdom comes from experience, and experience come from making mistakes."

" Walk by faith, not by sight."— 2 Corinthians 5:7

Please don't think you need to have all the answers before you start your business. Do Not Wait! There will be No Perfect Time! Start Now and here's how.

Business is built in real time-not from perfection, but from trial and error and courage. Don't be afraid to get it wrong. It simply sharpens your mind and skills and inadvertently builds a Boss.

If you have the dream, the desire, and the determination, everything else can be learned. The scripture *"Believe in things unseen as if they already are"* carried me through every chapter of my business journey, even when life made no sense. I can not say my mind was still enough to remember consciously visualizing Braids by SaBrina, but by the time Just-in-Time Barber shop and Inked 4 Life Tattoo Studio were born I knew the importance of seeing the dream in your minds eye first. Mind is All and every invention began with a image in the mind of its creator.

You can do this. Have faith in your vision. So grab your notepad, take a breath, and take notes. Do not depend on your memory. Write everything down, keep every receipt. Go get some cheap folders from Staples or The Dollar Tree. Keep a record of expense and income always.

Starting Without a Blueprint

When I began my business, I didn't have the internet, social media or Youtube University to learn from. There were no online marketing courses that I knew of. There was no search bar to ask: "How do I start a business?" "How do I get clients?" "How do I advertise?" "How do I get a business license?" I had NONE of that.

But you do and the internet is one of the greatest blessings a new entrepreneur can have today. Utilize it, it can help you build your business much faster than those starting years ago.

Don't abandon the old-school methods.

Do ALL of it. Old school, New school, Grassroots, Boots on the Ground (lol) hard work built Braids By SaBrina long before the digital world existed. You can not be lazy and build a successful business. Many times I was exhausted from braiding all day but I still hit up the parking lots near my home with flyers when i got off.

17

Small Local Newspapers Still Matter

One of the smartest early moves I made was buying ads in small community newspapers. Back then, a $45 ad could change EVERYTHING, and sometimes it did.

I took out adds in the La Sentinel, Scoop and the Wave news paper that was thrown in front of peoples houses in my West LA neighborhood. The News will never die. Newspapers still exist because people still read them.

Your ideal clients are everywhere. Meet them everywhere. Find Them !

- Place a small ad in the local city newspaper
- Attend local events and pass out your business cards
- Never turn away someone's business card or flyer, accept them graciously because you want people to accept yours.

Visibility is power—monopolize the market. When I opened my braiding salon in Los Angeles, there were only three other businesses similar to mine. You may not get that lucky. You may have chosen a business that has many competitors. Don't let that discourage you. It will be harder, but you were built for it. Do not shy away from one-on-one contact. Keep cards and flyers with you, and look people directly in their face with a big smile and say: "Excuse me, can I please give you one of my business cards?" If they say no—because some will—do not get in your feelings. Keep smiling and move on to the next.

Avoid My Early Mistakes

When you're new, everything looks like a great advertising opportunity. That's how I learned a hard lesson about paying huge amounts of money for others to direct-mail my flyers:

- There's no proof anything was ever mailed.
- There's no guarantee it reached the right people.
- Do not pay people to pass out your flyers unless you are following right behind them.
- Do not pay large companies to do direct mailing for you, because you will never know if they mailed it or not.

Until you can afford a staff, do the footwork yourself. Even then you still must govern over where your flyers are going. No one, even employees will care as much as you do about advertising your business.

Once I got older, even though I always had staff to help pass out the flyers, I enjoyed doing it myself. It gave me time to exercise and say my "I am rich in all areas of my life" affirmations. If my feet or legs started hurting, my affirmation would shift into: "My legs are strong, my legs are strong," over and over again until I finished whatever parking lot I was putting flyers out in. Remember, the cells in your body can hear you. Watch your words, even when you are tired. There is so much confidence and peace in doing things yourself—handing out your own flyers, placing your own cards in people's hands, smiling directly in people's faces, delivering your own promo, explaining in your own words what your business offers. **That** is where your entrepreneurial muscles grow.

Another lesson I learned is this: do not hire family and friends.

I understand the desire to give cousin Pookie a job and put a little money in his pocket. However, I have rarely seen it work out when you hire family and friends. Some, not all, but the people you are closest to often seem to have a sense of entitlement. They won't work as hard and they expect favors. It's not worth it, and I advise against it. It is what is referred to as a conflict of interest. If they get upset with you for not giving them a job, use that as your excuse: "Sorry, it's a conflict of interest," lol.

The Mistakes I Learned From

This chapter is called *Trial and Error* because the errors taught me just as much as the trials and I want YOU to avoid the mistakes that cost me time, money and peace.

Mistake #1: Being Too Friendly With My Employees

When I started, I was young - and so were many of my braiders. I didn't have a lot of family support, so I naturally connected with them as friends, sisters, and sometimes like peers.

Because of that, I blurred lines I didn't know were lines. We partied together and hung out together like friends. We stayed out late together at clubs dancing. We even took a trip to Belize together. It was fun, but when back at work, I expected them to treat me like I was their boss.

There a a few of my braiders that I grew to love like family, no doubt. I loved them and their children immensely. We had a lot of fun together. However when you have formed that type of bond with people you employ it is harder to reprimand or terminate them. They can not switch their emotions back

I didn't understand leadership. I didn't understand boundaries and didn't understand that proximity weakens authority when the lines are not clear.

You can be kind AND professional.
  You can be loving AND firm.
  You can lead WITH heart, but you must STILL lead.
  I learned that much later, but YOU don't have to.

Mistake #2: Not Saving My Money

I made a lot of money but nobody taught me about saving it. Now I refuse to lie and say I was ever broke and destitute because I was not. I always, from the time I was 22 years old had my own place and covered all my bills by myself and on time.

However I didn't understand wealth-building. I didn't understand financial discipline. I bought $500 purses and $300 glasses in those early years. I did at least buy a home in my 5th year of business and I paid off several luxury vehicles but I never saved simply for the sake of saving. I was never financially irresponsible. I was never one to be late on rent or bills at all. I just had not mastered saving.

I educated myself on how to buy a home from reading 'Home Buying for Dummies". I knew going in the door that I wanted: a 30 year fixed mortgage with no prepayment penalties. And that is exactly what I got. they were astonished at the little young twenty nine year old girl coming in there with a pen and pad, telling them exactly what she wanted.

Buying that home in 2000 solely changed my financial future forever. If you can acquire property, I urge you to do so. It is one of the only things that appreciates in value. I bought my home in 2000 for $190,000 and sold it in 2025 for $998,000. It was the best decision I ever made.

But if I could talk to my younger self, I would tell her:

"Save more, Invest more, respect your money more", "Buy income property," and "Do not trade your car in for a newer model every time you pay in off".

If you're starting a business today:

- Open a savings account (and do not touch it)
- Get a life insurance policy on yourself and your children and never let it laps
- Don't finance a vehicle and get a huge payment and high interest rate
- Open a CD (certificate of deposit account) and let it sit for 5 years
- Don't waste money on designer purses and shoes
- Never tell people how much money you make
- Pay your business taxes quarterly
- Save $20 from ever $100

Your future self will thank you. Discipline is key. Pay yourself a specific amount and save the rest for a rainy day.

What I Did Do Right: Teaching Financial Literacy

I did a lot right. Even though I didn't save nearly as much money as I should have, I made sure my braiders learned everything I did.

I used to take them to Broadway Federal Bank on Venice Blvd

in Los Angeles and help them open their own bank accounts. I had my financial adviser come and do a presentation for them about short and long term investing.

I created my own short and long term stock portfolio with a company that used to be called TD Waterhouse. I educated myself on every stock in the Dow Jones Industrial Average.

When it came to my home, I also learned a "Dummie" book, to always pay additional money towards your principal ONLY. Make sure to stipulate that on your check or money order or the finance company will not apply it solely to the principal balance.

I am writing this book in 2025 and sharing this information in a book, but I have always shared it with whomever would listen. I always told the young women who worked for me to work and learn from me for two to three years then go out and open their own business. I planted seeds in their financial future — and many of them still thank me for it.

Mistake #3: Not Paying Taxes for Two Years

This is a mistake that will humble you FAST. I made the mistake of not paying taxes for two years — and the trouble that followed was stressful, frightening, and completely avoidable.

Here's my advice, so listen well: DO NOT AVOID THE IRS! Handle your taxes. All of them, on time.

I had a bad habit of ignoring things I didn't understand or tossing aside mail that overwhelmed me. DO NOT DO THAT! The Internal Revenue Service must be paid. If you don't understand it, then do as I did and hire a licensed tax professional. They will help you:

- To arrange quarterly payments

- File taxes every single year
- Keep organized receipts
- Clean bookkeeping
- Create a paper trail

Don't wait for the IRS to remind you. Learn from me, you can thank me later.

Hard Lessons, but Grateful I learned them.

1. Friendships and business rarely mix. Set boundaries early. You can NOT be a friend and a Boss.
2. Save at least 10–20% of every dollar you earn.
3. Pay your taxes - the IRS does not forget you.
4. Don't depend solely on digital marketing - combine new and old-school methods.
5. Don't spend everything you make because busy seasons don't last forever.
6. Hire slow, fire quick, Let go of any employee that is a threat to your business
7. Your business will only grow to the level of your discipline.

The Beauty of Trial and Error

Starting a business isn't about being perfect - it's about being willing to learn. Your mistakes will shape you. Your missteps will guide you. Your failures will teach you. Your determination will refine you.

Your own experience will be your greatest teacher - but me

sharing my experiences with you can save you from the pain that comes with avoidable lessons. That's why I wrote this book.....So that each of YOU can experience the freedom of self-employment.

www.braidsbysabrina.com/wsj.htm

Get Out of Her Hair

SaBrina Reese is a 28-year-old entrepreneur who owns two African hair-braiding salons. In July, the state of California mounted an elaborate sting operation and cited her for not having a cosmetology license. Ms. Reese says the law requiring that hair-braiders have such a license is a relic of the "Jim Crow" era and she is fighting it in court.

Ms. Reese began braiding hair in high school and actually went to cosmetology school for a while. But braiding was neither included in the curriculum nor tested in the licensing exam, so she decided the 1,600 hours and $9,000 the school required were useless to her. Because her shops only braid hair and don't use chemicals, it makes little sense to require her to learn how to, for example, curl hair.

SaBrina Reese

She says the state cosmetology board, which sent two people to her shop on July 1 to entrap her, is simply trying to shut down competition at the behest of other beauty shop owners. Indeed, one owner told the Los Angeles Times that entrepreneurs such as Ms. Reese are "a threat to those of us who are licensed and went through the normal channels."

When Ms. Reese wanted to open her first shop, she went down to City Hall and asked officials what she needed. They told her to get a professional occupations license and a commercial business license, both of which she now has hanging on her wall. They said nothing about a cosmetology license. Her business thrived, she opened a second location and she now has nine employees.

Then last year, she was fined more than $1,000 by the state cosmetology board. She appealed the fine and had it reduced to $500. Last month, a state investigator pretending to be a customer entered her store and cited her and her employees for practicing "cosmetology" without a license. Ms. Reese faces a possible one-year jail sentence, but city prosecutors have declined to pursue the case for now, pending the outcome of a similar case in San Diego set to go to trial. Ms. Reese hopes the law being used against her will be thrown out as a result of a federal civil rights suit brought by the Institute for Justice. One of the plaintiffs is JoAnne Cornwell, a professor at San Diego State University, who says the anti-hair-braiding law "stifles the entrepreneurial urge in the community." The entrepreneurial urge is indeed common to the human spirit, and we don't doubt there are many more such as SaBrina Reese in the nation's cities who'd thrive if freed of such restrictions and burdens.

Article written about me by the Wall Street Journal

Braids By SaBrina Staff in 1999

During a documentary about the life of SaBrina Fisher Reece

SaBrina's 3 daughters Joi, Jayden and Journey learning to Braid

3

Guerrilla Marketing-Flooding the City With Your Name

One thing about me: when it came to marketing, I didn't play. I believed in **being everywhere,** and I mean *everywhere.*

For years, I ordered **5,000 flyers at a time** from VistaPrint and NextDayFlyers. My staff and I would pile into my big burgundy H2 Hummer, windows down, music on, and we'd turn the entire city of Los Angeles into a walking billboard for Braids By SaBrina.

I advertised at malls, churches, swap meets, colleges, grocery stores, movie theaters, community events and more. If there were people there, my flyers were there.

If you parked your car at any of Los Angeles annual, popular event like: Taste of Soul, Gardena Jazz Fest. Universe Soul Circus, concerts at the Forum. I was there either with my staff, my kids or alone passing out my fliers.

A System So Good, It Was a Science

I even mastered the art of placing a flyer on a car without setting off the alarm, and once I learned it, I trained my whole staff. Even my children grew up putting out flyers with me. That was their version of "after-school activities," and they didn't even realize they were learning entrepreneurship before they could spell the word.

And let me be clear: It didn't matter if I had been in business **5, 10, 15, 20 years,** I *never* stopped marketing this way. Real entrepreneurs understand that visibility is a lifestyle, not a phase. Yes, I monopolized all of the free internet marketing as well but I never stopped Guerrilla Marketing, and you should not either.

Fence & Pole Signs: My Trademark Stamp on the City

Then came the **fence & pole signs,** the ones people *still* remember to this day. Initially I used make my signs by hand, then later upgraded to **professionally printed fluorescent pink signs** big enough and bright enough to catch the eye of any driver from half a block away. Fluorescent pink wasn't just a color, it was a *strategy*. You couldn't miss it if you tried.

I kept a **staple gun** and in the truck at all times. Actually, we kept several, along with zip ties, tape, backup hardware, and stacks of signs, fliers and business cards.

My Hummer stayed stocked like a mobile advertising command center. We would hop out, staple a sign to a pole in seconds, jump back in, and move on to the next corner.

Efficiency. Speed. Precision. We were a whole guerrilla marketing unit.

Marketing Was Never Optional — But It Was Always Fun

Now let me be honest, I'm a Leo, so there was no "maybe" when it came to advertising. It was mandatory if you worked for me. We were going out, period. If i was dating someone, he would help with the advertising as well. But I always made it fun. We laughed, we talked, we bonded, and we built something together. Marketing wasn't a chore, it was an adventure. And because we did it together, my staff took pride in it. They understood that this is what brings the customers to the salon. The staff weren't just braiders; they were part of the movement that built Braids By SaBrina into an empire.

Always Ready. Always Hustling. Always Prepared.

I kept my truck stocked because I understood something early:
A business owner must always be ready for opportunity.
If I saw a fence — I had zip ties.
If I saw a wooden pole — I had staples.
If I saw a crowded parking lot — I had flyers.
If I saw a high-traffic corner — I had signs.
I didn't wait for customers to just find me.
I went out and found *them*.

That "make it happen" spirit? That wasn't learned, that was God-given. No one taught me to hustle that hard. No one sat me down and explained marketing strategy. I didn't grow up around entrepreneurs. I took a couple of business management classes at West LA College but what I learned about small business came from hands on work.
Something in me just **knew**.

Knew what to do.

Knew how to do it.

Knew how to outwork, out think, and out-hustle anyone standing in my way.

That instinct - that fire - built a business that lasted over **30 years**.

My famous Florescent Pink "Braids By SaBrina" Signs

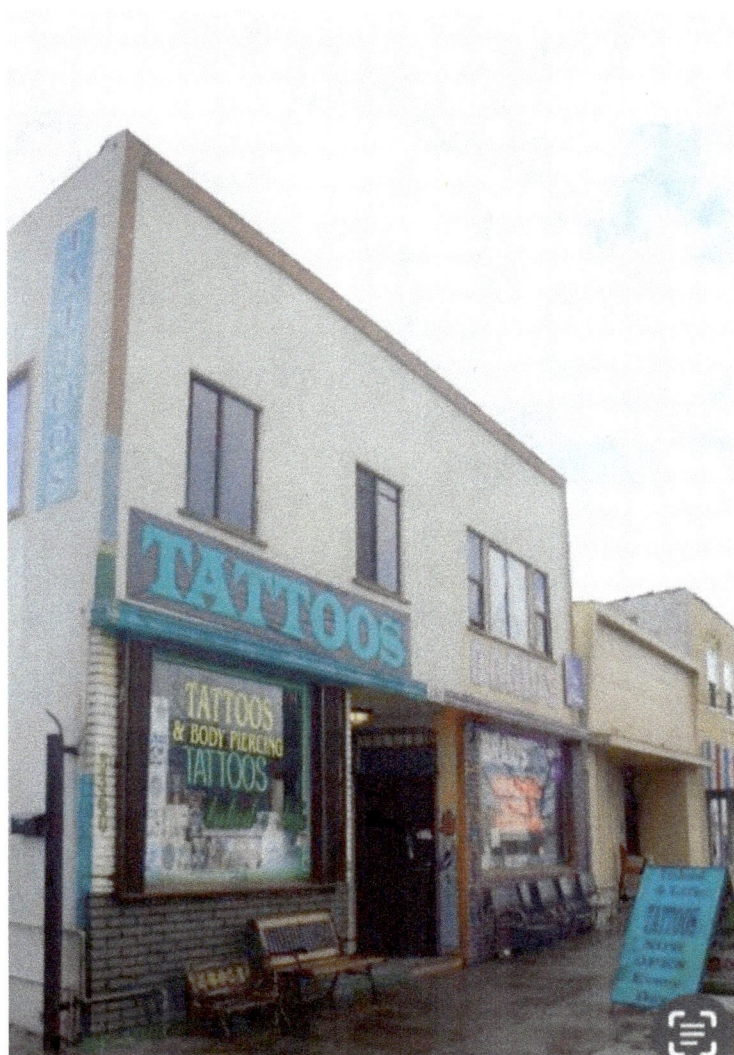

My Tattoo Shop "Inked 4 Life Tattoo Studio"

Braiding Staff when we all wore Heather Gray

When I transitioned the Salon from "Braids By SaBrina" to "A New Vision Dreadlock Studio

Advertisement for my publishing company in 2026

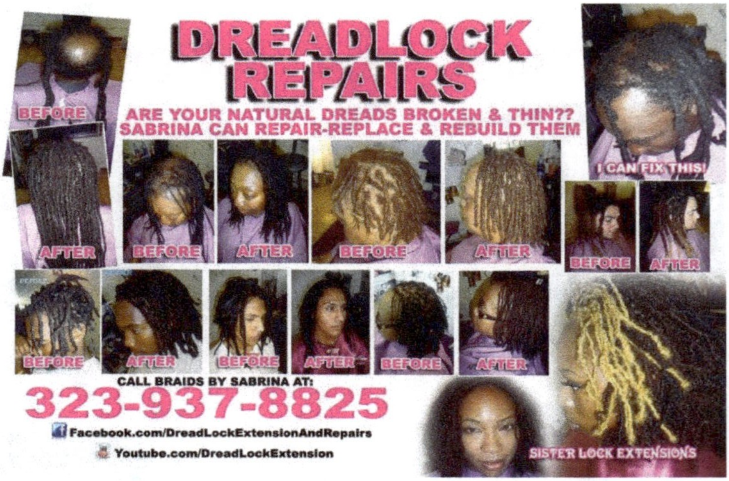

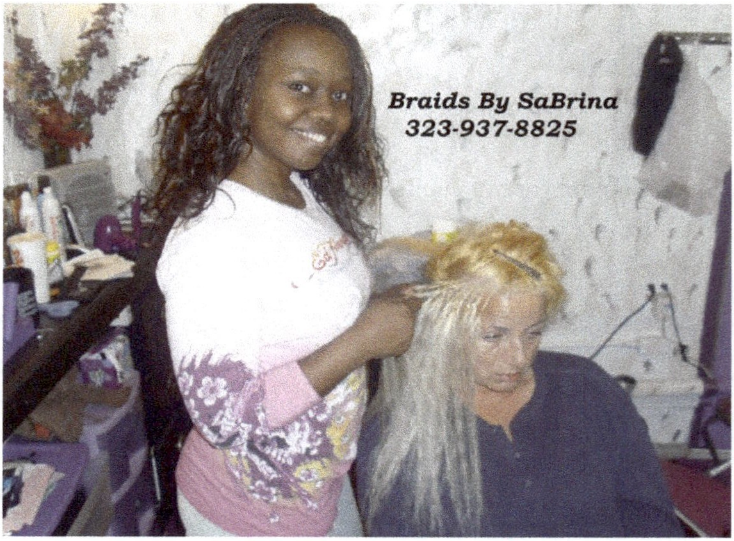

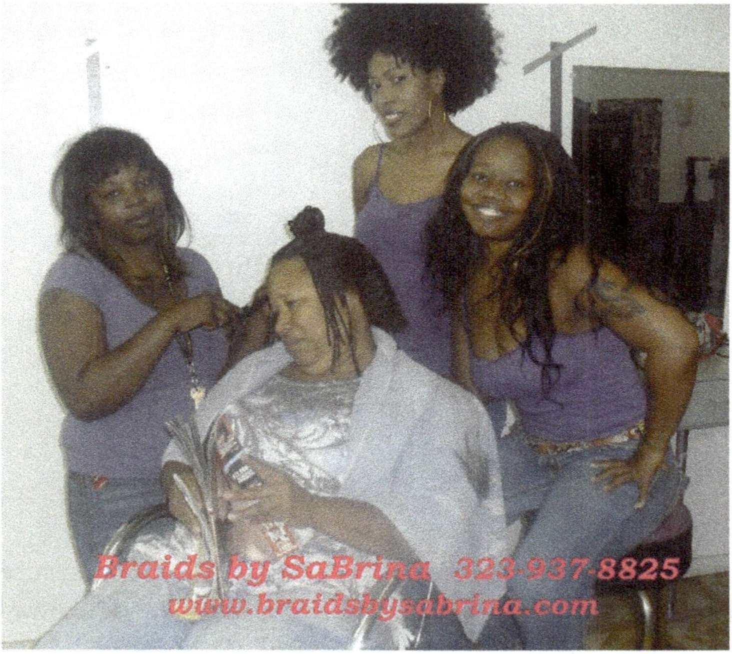
Braids by SaBrina 323-937-8825
www.braidsbysabrina.com

4

Building Relationships

Make no mistake, I wasn't always good at building relationships. In the beginning, I had one speed: **my way or the highway.** I even had signs in the salon that said exactly that. At just **5'2"**, still drowning in unprocessed trauma, I was like a little chihuahua, small, loud, and fiercely protective of myself.

But even in those early days, I was a **teacher** at heart. I poured into my staff the same way I wished someone had poured into me. I taught them that *they could start a business too.* I'd tell them, "Learn from me for a few years, then go open your own business".

When I learned about mutual funds, savings accounts, and certificates of deposit accounts, I brought that knowledge right back to the salon. I reminded them often, *"Twenty dollars is still worth saving."* I wanted them to break generational patterns, not just braid hair.

Over the years, more than 1,700 women, and five very interesting men, worked for me. At any given time, I managed between six and eleven braiders, each coming to my salon with a different story and a different struggle. Some were fighting addiction, some were battling life's storms, some were carrying quiet pain they never spoke about, and some were simply trying to hold their lives together one day at a time. I hired, fired, and rehired over 70% of my staff because I always believed in giving people another chance, even when the world had already counted them out. I had staff who plotted against me, who tried to rob me, who let envy twist into intentions to harm me, but through it all, I survived. I survived because this wasn't just a business; it was my calling. It was the gift God placed in my hands, and His protection covered me every step of the way.

I ran a tight ship. They had to be on time, and I never compromised on quality. My name was on that door, and I insisted that every braid reflected excellence. When something went wrong, My name "SaBrina" was who the client looked to complain to. So I was very consistent with making sure my staff maintained my motto of professionalism.

I've had a braider walk out with $860 of my money. But even those painful moments came with lessons. I had gotten too comfortable and trusted the wrong people, something every new business owner eventually experiences.

The truth is, I was learning and growing right alongside them. I was only **26 years old** when I opened my salon. I kept expecting my staff to think like me, work like me, and care like me, but they weren't me. They didn't share my hustle or my urgency, and they weren't supposed to. Many of them were ambitious but I reminded them that I did not build "Braids By SaBrina" by Stealing from someone else.

Everything I went through shaped me into the leader I eventually became, firm, fair, compassionate, and finally at peace. I'm still a boss, but I am much softer now than I was then. I always loved my braiders, probably got way too involved in their personal lives, but eventually, I learned how to set healthy boundaries.

Over three decades, I hired hundreds of Belizeans, many Africans from Senegal, Cameroon, the Congo, and more. Some were absolute sweethearts. Others were only there for the money. Either way, I wish every single one of them the best.

Because together, through mistakes, growth, arguments, laughter, and years of learning, we built something powerful. Real relationships are not perfect. But they are the heartbeat of every successful business.

Leadership isn't only about the business decisions you make. Sometimes it's the prayers God puts in your mouth on behalf of the women you're called to lead.

JoAnn and Sade working at "Braids By SaBrina"

Teaching a Braiding Class

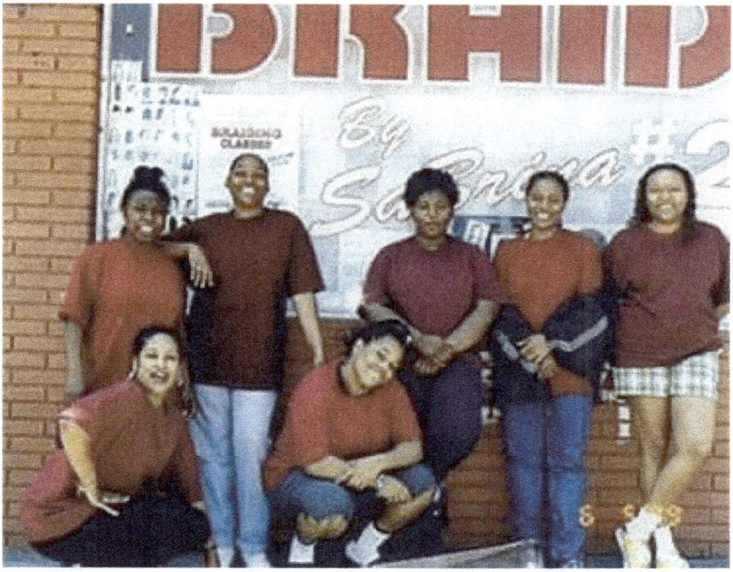
By

Braids By SaBrina Staff

Braids By SaBrina Staff on Adams Blvd

Inked 4 Life Tattoo Studio · Join

SaBrina Fisher Reece · Nov 6, 2009 · 🌐

Offering discounts at INKED 4 LIFE TATTOO STUDIO to USC Students !...Must bring USC Student ID to receive discount......5360 W. Adams

my Tattoo Shop and some of my tattoo artist

Velma. Audrey & SaBrina headed to a R Kelly concert

Braids By SaBrina when I ran out of space and rented the building right next door so I could hire more Braiders

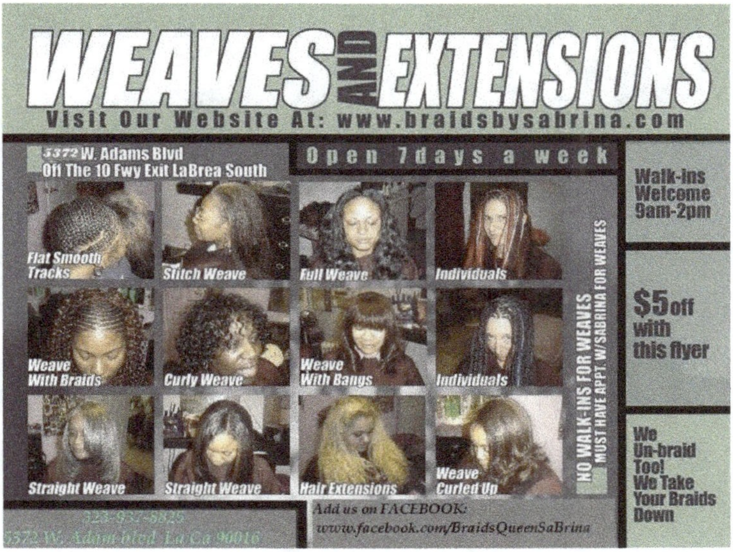

One of my many Braids By SaBrina postcards

Braids By SaBrina on Adams blvd

Braids By SaBrina 323-937-8825
www.braidsbysabrina.com

5

Structure, Standards & Standing Your Ground

Every successful business eventually reaches a crossroads: Either you train your clients... or your clients train you.

In the early years of Braids By SaBrina, I learned this lesson the hard way. I wanted to please everyone, I understood single mothers trying to pull money together, women dealing with breakups, or people simply trying to keep their heads above water. But understanding does not mean allowing chaos. If you want your business to last, you must create structure.

I quickly learned that if I wanted consistency, respect, and financial stability, I had to set policies that protected my time, my staff, and my peace. Not everyone liked it, but everyone needed it. The women I pushed to follow a schedule may not have understood it at the time, but that discipline became a positive trait they would carry into their daily lives. I realized early on that if you don't assign specific times for staff to show up, they will stroll in whenever they want. That's why I created a system: the first braider to arrive got the first client. That simple rule taught responsibility, rewarded effort, and kept the entire salon running smoothly.

Creating Real Policies in a Real-World Business

Braiding is intimate work. Clients tell you their secrets, they bring you their emotions, their children, their stories. But what they cannot bring is disrespect, manipulation, or attempts to avoid paying.

I had clients who would try everything:

- "Can you just braid half today and I'll pay the rest Friday?"
- "My boyfriend is on his way with the money."
- "My check didn't hit yet... can you spot me?"
- "I forgot my money, but I'll Cash App you later."
- "But I'm your regular!"

No ma'am. No sir. This is where my strong Leo personality served me well in the salon. I did not play about my money, and you should not play about yours. That doesn't mean you have to be rude, you can request payment kindly and in a soft voice, but you should never continue working until you receive it.

It's also not fair to leave clients confused about your expectations, so always let them know what forms of payment you accept and *when* you will be requesting it. The best way is to provide your policies in advance. Send a text or email that clearly states something like: "Full payment is required in advance, shortly after we begin, or halfway through, whichever aligns best with your business."

This is a business — not a charity, not a hobby, and definitely not a love offering.

So I implemented rules that protected the salon:

✔ Deposits required. No exceptions. (In later years, I did not require deposits at first)
  ✔ Payment before service completion.
  ✔ No last-minute cancellations without fees.
  ✔ No "friend discounts."
  ✔ No price haggling.
  ✔ Price list visible and consistent.

The moment I enforced these rules with consistency, the entire energy of the salon shifted. People treat you the way you allow them to treat you, and when you stand firm in your standards, the right clients will rise to meet them.

Protecting My Staff Like a Mama Lion

I always had a team, sometimes 6 braiders, sometimes 11. These girls were young, many came from tough homes, some battling their own traumas. I knew that if anything happened to them on my watch, I would never forgive myself.

That is why I adopted a strict **locked-door policy**.
  Even if the sun was shining...
  Even if the neighborhood seemed quiet...
  Even if clients didn't understand...
  The door stayed locked.
  No walk-ins wandering in. We had to open the door for you.
  No men "looking for directions."
  No strange, friends and family could sit inside salon with

58

client

Not on my watch.

I was responsible for those women, their safety, and their ability to go home to their families. A locked door saved us many times, situations we will never even know we avoided. Most salons are cash based businesses. Keep your Doors Locked!

Scheduling With Wisdom

People think braiders work endlessly. And some do, but not mine. I braided hair in my home on 109th in Normandie for a couple of years before my salon opened. My schedule then was more flexible because I was at home. Once I opened the salon I had to adhere to a set schedule.

I built a schedule I was proud of: **4 days on, 3 days off.** Rotating shifts. Predictable hours. Space to breathe. Sometimes the girls would switch days with each other.

Yes, there were nights we worked until midnight, especially prom season, holidays, graduation time, summer vacations, but those nights were teamwork nights. We laughed, ate, and teamed up together on one head.

Balancing Compassion With Boundaries

You can love your clients. You can love your staff. You can be kind, warm, spiritual, and generous......but you must also be unshakably firm.

If you don't control your business, the business, and everyone in it, will end up controlling you.

And the most powerful lesson I ever learned as a businesswoman?

Kindness needs boundaries, and boundaries build empires.

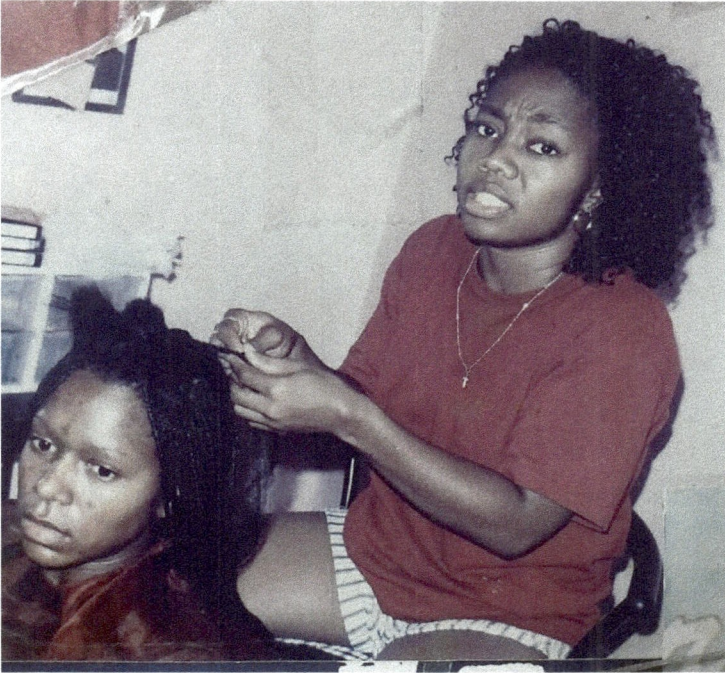

The Braid Queen SaBrina

Me and some of my braiders posing before a trip to Magic Mountain

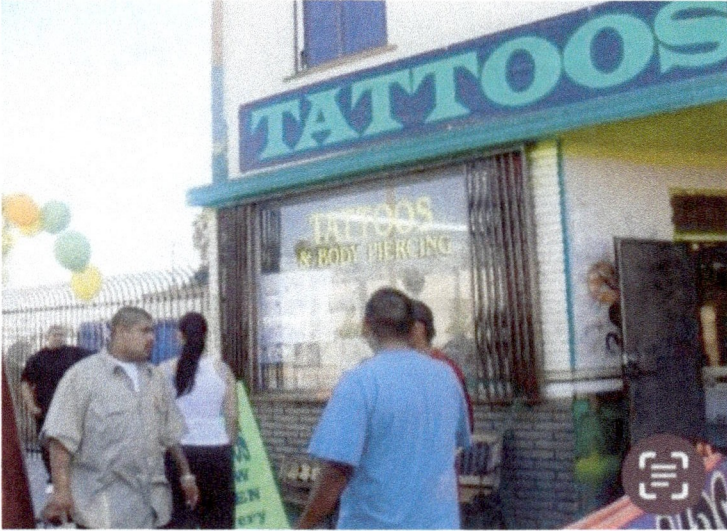

Some of my Tattoo Artist outside my shop on Adams Blvd

My Braids By SaBrina Staff in 2004. My daughters Joi and Jayden are the little girls in picture

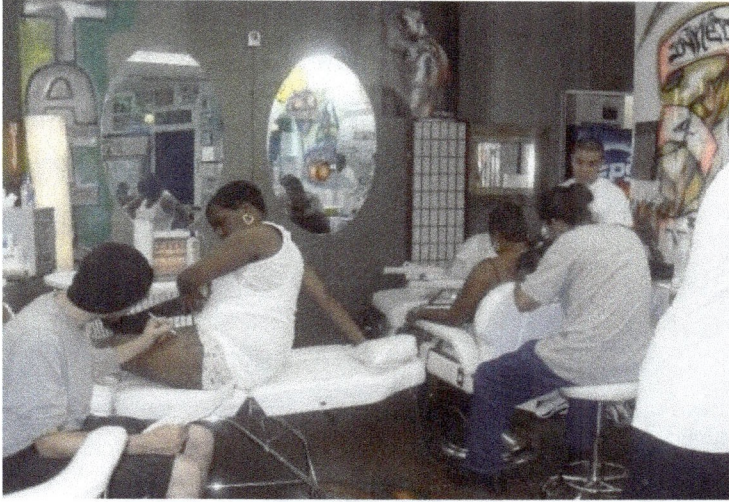

Inside my Tattoo shop "Inked 4 Life Tattoo Studio"

An Advertisement for my tattoo shop Inked 4 Life

Braids By SaBrina Braiders working hard

6

Leadership With Heart: The Art of Being the Boss

I didn't become a leader because I wanted to be one. I became a leader because life demanded it. When you run a salon for 30 years, you don't just braid hair, you braid lives, stories, cultures, personalities, traumas, and dreams.

Leadership became my destiny. I am now certain that God created me just for this.

Leading Women From Every Walk of Life

I hired over **1,700 women** during my career, and five unforgettable men.

They came from everywhere:

- Belize
- Senegal
- Cameroon

- Congo
- South L.A.
- Inglewood
- Gardena
- Watts
- Compton

Some were sweet. Many were broken like me. Some were brilliant. Some were chaotic. A Few were gang affiliated and others were thieves. Some were simply trying to survive. But all of them were searching for a chance. I honored to have been able to offer them that chance.

Building The Salon Culture

When you walked into Braids By SaBrina, you didn't just enter a salon — you stepped into a world with its own heartbeat, its own energy, its own expectations, and its own rhythm. That space was sacred to me. I built a culture rooted in:

✔ **Excellence** — every braid mattered because every woman and man mattered.

✔ **Timeliness** — you don't stroll in at 12 when your shift starts at 11; that was my way of teaching responsibility and respect.

✔ **Respect** — not just for clients, but for each other, because many of us came from places where respect wasn't freely given.

✔ **Accountability** — you don't disappear for hours or leave in the middle of a style; people were trusting us with their crowns.

✔ **Sisterhood** — we uplift each other, not compete, because life had already given many of us enough battles.

Did everyone follow these rules? Of course not. Many times, clients thought the behavior of my braiders was ghetto, and truthfully, sometimes we all were a little ghetto. Our attitudes weren't always the best, but we were young, growing, learning, healing, and trying to figure life out. As I grew, they grew, and we became better women together.

But one thing the clients could never deny, **we could braid our butts off.** No matter what chaos was happening behind the scenes, the work was always masterpieces.

When customers brought issues to me, I dealt with them head-on. I fired and rehired at least 80% of my staff at one time or another.

Why? Because I believed in second chances, and truth be told, many of us survived life because someone believed in *us* when we didn't deserve it. Sometimes my staff needed structure. Sometimes they needed love. Sometimes they needed another chance just to prove to themselves that they could do better. I have never been one to hold grudges. By The time some of them would return to ask for their jobs back, I had forgotten why they were fired anyway.

In the end, Braids By SaBrina became a household name because of the standard I set, and because I refused to lower the bar, even on the days when life felt heavy. The quality of work I demanded wasn't just about braids. It was about pride, purpose, and knowing that even if the world counted us out, inside those salon walls, we were building something powerful.

The Hard Lessons of Being the Boss

Being a leader is not glamorous. People will test you. People will steal from you. People will sit in your business and talk about you. People will betray you, and trust me — I have experienced it all.

I've had someone walk straight out with my money. I've had a staff member try to set me up to be robbed. I've witnessed employees create drama, lies, jealousy, and sabotage. I've had people mistake my kindness for weakness. I've had clients try to run game on me about paying for their services. You name it I've been through it. But I'm not mad, I hold not even one grudge. I wish them all the best.

There was a time when I was running "Braids By SaBrina" salon and school *and* "Inked for Life Tattoo Studio" at the same time. And if you think it's difficult getting young women to follow the rules, try managing young men. It's far more challenging. Imagine grown, 6'2" tattoo artists having to follow my lead and then pay me 40%. It wasn't easy — but it taught me something powerful: **I can run any business.**

Every lesson sharpened me.

Every betrayal strengthened me.

Every hardship refined my leadership.

And through it all, I became exactly who I was meant to be.

Learning to Lead With Compassion

I opened my business at 26. Back then, in my 20s, I was a firecracker, all bark, all bite. Not because I was mean, but because I was hurting. Pain can harden you without you even realizing it. But as I grew spiritually, emotionally, and mentally, something beautiful happened: I softened, and I did it without ever losing my strength.

I learned how to listen with compassion.

How to forgive without forgetting my worth.

How to encourage women who were carrying silent battles.

How to inspire people simply by showing up as myself.

How to create boundaries that honored my peace.

How to be a firm leader with a nurturing, mother-like presence.

I stopped yelling and started teaching. Many of my braiders will never forget when they saw that change in me. I stopped reacting out of old wounds and started guiding out of wisdom. I stopped trying to control everything and instead began empowering everyone. It happened right around the time I stepped into my purpose as a motivational speaker, when God began showing me that my voice had power beyond the salon.

And guess what? My salon flourished. People had always respected me as a fierce businesswoman, but now they respected me for something much deeper, for opening my heart, for letting them see my healing journey, and for showing them that they, too, could rise from whatever pain, trauma, or brokenness they were carrying.

I didn't just teach them how to braid.

I taught them how to believe again, in themselves, in their future, and in their own healing.

The Beauty of Leadership

Being a boss taught me:

- patience
- empathy
- resilience
- responsibility
- and unconditional love for the women who stood beside me

We learned and grew together. I made many mistakes as a young business owner. But the relationship we built were priceless.

Many of those women went on to open their own businesses, build families, travel the world, and leave the welfare system behind — and they still tell me I changed their lives.

But the truth is...

They changed mine, too.

Audrey, SaBrina, Lashanna, Barbara

Setting up for a Braiding Class

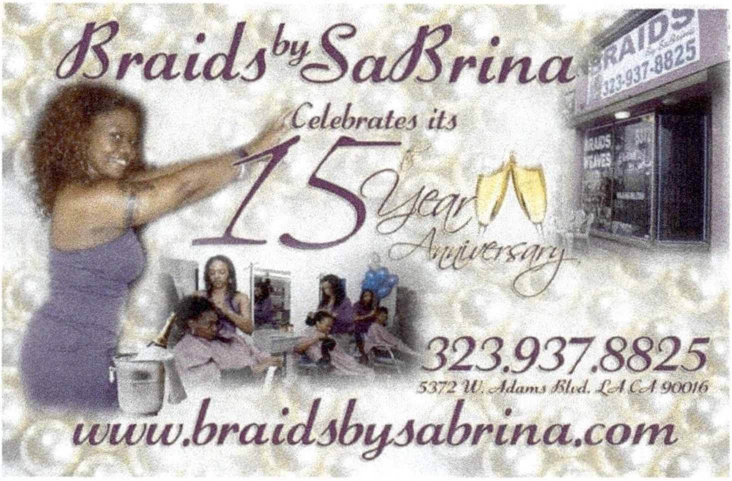

Braids By SaBrina's 15th Anniversary Flyer

Receiving and award for my contribution to the City as a business owner from Jan Perry

City of
Los Angeles
State of California
RESOLUTION
Braids by SaBrina

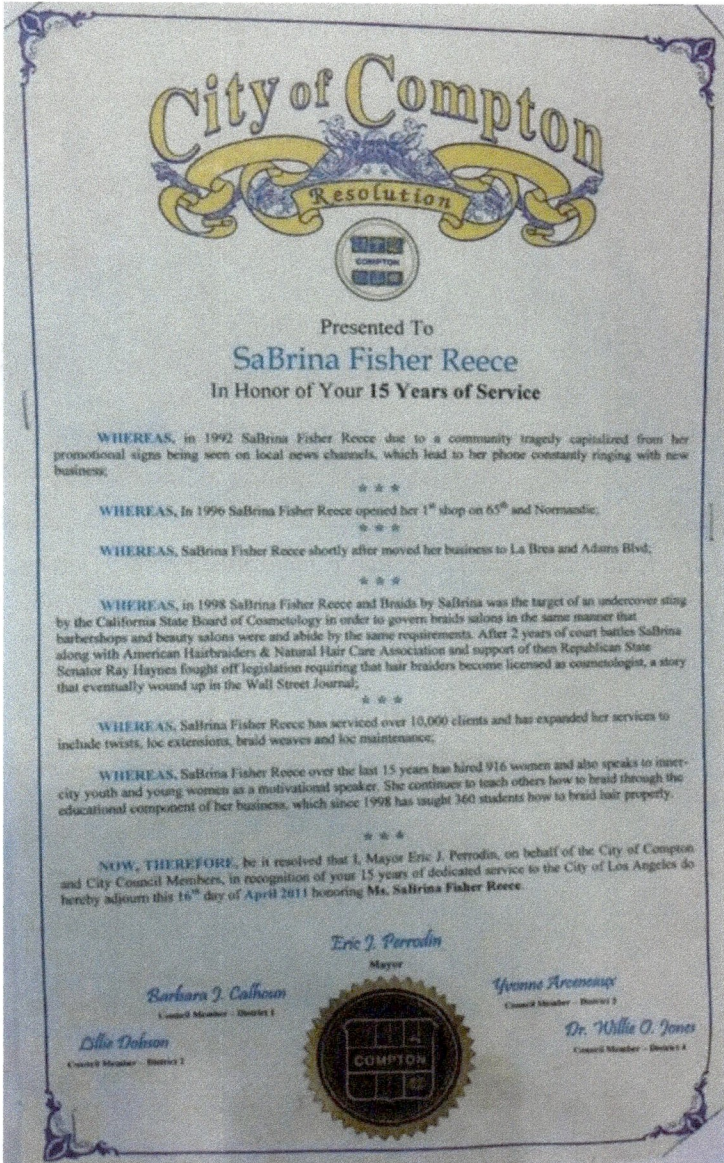

City of Compton
Resolution

Presented To
SaBrina Fisher Reece
In Honor of Your **15 Years of Service**

WHEREAS, in 1992 SaBrina Fisher Reece due to a community tragedy capitalized from her promotional signs being seen on local news channels, which lead to her phone constantly ringing with new business;

* * *

WHEREAS, In 1996 SaBrina Fisher Reece opened her 1st shop on 65th and Normandie;

* * *

WHEREAS, SaBrina Fisher Reece shortly after moved her business to La Brea and Adams Blvd;

* * *

WHEREAS, in 1998 SaBrina Fisher Reece and Braids by SaBrina was the target of an undercover sting by the California State Board of Cosmetology in order to govern braids salons in the same manner that barbershops and beauty salons were and abide by the same requirements. After 2 years of court battles SaBrina along with American Hairbraiders & Natural Hair Care Association and support of then Republican State Senator Ray Haynes fought off legislation requiring that hair braiders become licensed as cosmetologist, a story that eventually wound up in the Wall Street Journal;

* * *

WHEREAS, SaBrina Fisher Reece has serviced over 10,000 clients and has expanded her services to include twists, loc extensions, braid weaves and loc maintenance;

WHEREAS, SaBrina Fisher Reece over the last 15 years has hired 916 women and also speaks to inner-city youth and young women as a motivational speaker. She continues to teach others how to braid through the educational component of her business, which since 1998 has taught 360 students how to braid hair properly.

* * *

NOW, THEREFORE, be it resolved that I, Mayor Eric J. Perrodin, on behalf of the City of Compton and City Council Members, in recognition of your 15 years of dedicated service to the City of Los Angeles do hereby adjourn this 16th day of **April 2011** honoring **Ms. SaBrina Fisher Reece**.

Eric J. Perrodin
Mayor

Barbara J. Calhoun
Council Member - District 1

Yvonne Arceneaux
Council Member - District 3

Lillie Dobson
Council Member - District 2

Dr. Willie O. Jones
Council Member - District 4

79

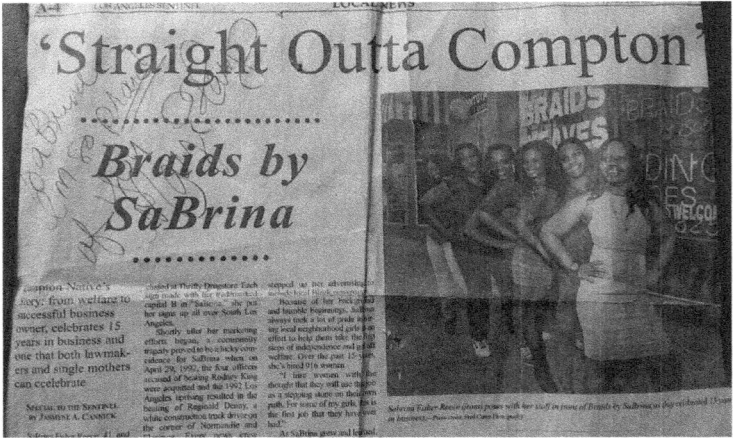

Article about SaBrina Fisher Reece and signed by Mary Harvey

SaBrina & Colletta

7

Practical Tools to Build, Grow & Sustain Your Business

Once you've found your purpose and built your foundation, it's time to begin the real work: **execution**.

People love the idea of owning a business, but it's the daily disciplines, those consistent, taxing, un-glamorous habits, that separate dreamers from doers. Don't just talk about it, Be About it!

This chapter gives you the **exact habits and systems** I used to build a 30-year business from nothing but braid extensions, grit, and God-given imagination. These steps are simple. They are doable. And if you commit to them, your business will grow.

1. Set Times for Consistent Advertising

Marketing is not an "every now and then" job—it is the lifeline of your business.

In my salon days, I didn't wait for clients to "just show up."

I went after them. I placed fliers directly in their hands.
Today's entrepreneur MUST create a marketing rhythm.
▶ **Set a daily timer on your phone**
Advertising is like brushing your teeth, do it every single day.

- 15 minutes posting on social media
- 20 minutes responding to inquiries
- 10 minutes promoting a service
- 1–2 hours a week distributing physical fliers

Small daily actions add up to big business momentum.

2. Visualize Your Success Every Day

Visualization is not "wishful thinking" it is strategy.
Before Braids By SaBrina ever opened, I saw it in my mind.
I saw:

- women smiling in my chairs
- the phone ringing nonstop
- my staff working confidently
- the colors I wanted the Braiders to wear
- money flowing
- my salon full and thriving

You MUST see it before you live it.
▶ **Spend 5 minutes a day visualizing your business as if it already exists.**
Sit still, close your eyes, breathe deeply, and imagine:

- your storefront

- your products
- your clients
- your income
- your joy

"Your imagination is God's gift, the place where you see the unseen until it becomes real. Faith is believing in what you cannot see as if it already exists." Hebrews 11:1 (KJV)

"Now faith is the substance of things hoped for, the evidence of things not seen."

3. Write Everything Down & Stay Organized

A successful business starts with **paper and a plan**.
   You do NOT need a fancy office or a business master's degree.
You simply need:

- a notebook
- a binder
- a calendar
- a folder system
- a plan

Write down:

- expenses
- marketing ideas
- supplies needed
- weekly goals
- long-term vision

- client notes
- policies

And YES, **collect every client's email and phone number.**
Keep that list updated.
Your email list is your goldmine.
▶ **Create a folder for every part of your business:**

- Finances
- Marketing
- Inventory
- Services
- Policies
- Employee paperwork
- Vision & goals

Organization creates clarity. Clarity creates confidence. Confidence creates profit.

4. Be Kinder Than You've Ever Been

Kindness is not weakness—it is strategy.
I learned that a smile can turn a $50 client into a $500 client because they trust you, they feel safe with you, and they want to return.
People remember:

- how you treated them
- how you spoke to them
- how you made them feel

Kindness builds loyalty faster than any advertisement.
Make it your mission to:

- greet clients warmly
- compliment them genuinely
- shake their hand
- say "thank you"
- look them in the eye and smile
- give encouragement

Kindness is free, but it pays like gold.

5. Do Not Abandon Old-School Marketing

Modern entrepreneurs rely too heavily on social media and forget the grind that truly builds a business.
Let me be clear:
Flyers still work.
Business cards still work.
Face-to-face networking STILL works.
I built an empire with flyers, signs, and footwork.
That method will never stop working.

▶ **Attend local events:**

- Farmer's markets
- Street fairs
- Beauty expos
- PTA meetings
- High school games
- Community gatherings

People trust the businesses they see in real life.

6. Dominate the Internet

Old school + new school = **unstoppable.**
You must monopolize the free resources at your fingertips.
Post everywhere:

- Instagram
- TikTok
- Facebook
- YouTube Shorts
- Google Business
- Pinterest
- Nextdoor
- Yelp
- Local business directories

You don't need to go viral, you only need to be consistent.
▶ **Create a schedule:**

- Post 1–2 times a day
- Respond to all messages within 24 hours
- Share client photos
- Show behind-the-scenes
- Give tips
- Share transformations
- Use tags and hashtags

Let the world know you exist, and they WILL find you.

Final Word for This Chapter

Building a business is not magic, but your mind, your discipline, and your consistency ARE. If you commit to these habits, you will grow. If you apply these steps daily, you will evolve. And if you show up with integrity, kindness, and hustle...**your business will thrive in ways you couldn't imagine.**

We always dressed up for holidays at Braid By SaBrina

Hair braiders, backers battle for right to work

by Charlene Muhammad

LOS ANGELES—The American Hairbraiders & Natural Haircare Association, the Congress of Racial Equality (CORE) and the Los Angeles County Black Chamber of Commerce hosted a community forum Oct. 25 to share proposed legislation that would end regulation of hair braiding.

"We're concerned with some of the attitudes and actions regarding some of the cultural things that we are involved in, and we want to see to it that those cultural things continue," said CORE State Chairman Celes King, III. He believes state licensing for hairbraiding is unnecessary, particularly since the craft is natural and has been performed by Blacks for years.

"We've always done it this way. It's just one sister helping out another sister and the fact that they get a gratuity or tip for it doesn't mean that it warrants becoming licensed," he added.

Joining the braiders, community, religious and political leaders at CORE headquarters to discuss the unfair regulation was California State Senator Raymond N. Hayes, who authored SB 235—the "Hairbraiding Licensure Exemption." Mr. Haynes feels government involvement in hairbraiding is inappropriate and he

SaBrina Reese (at right with supporter Calif. State Senator Raymond N. Hayes), who owns a braiding salon, was arrested by state regulators for practicing her craft. She and her staff (above) hope a new bill that would eliminate state oversight passes the California legislature.

Photos: Charlene Muhammad

government coming in and arresting braiders. Mr. Haynes said

government assistance. Our community for a long time has not been

A Article in the Final Call newspaper

90

Natalie Cole was a client of mine for years.

Braids by SaBrina staff in 2003

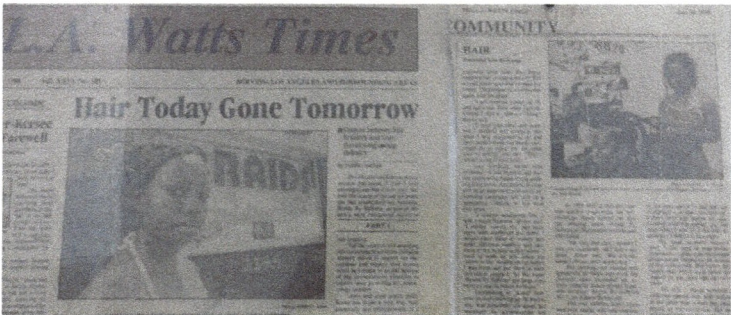

Article written about Braids By SaBrina in the L.A. Watts Times

When I first began speaking motivationally, my braiders were my first audience

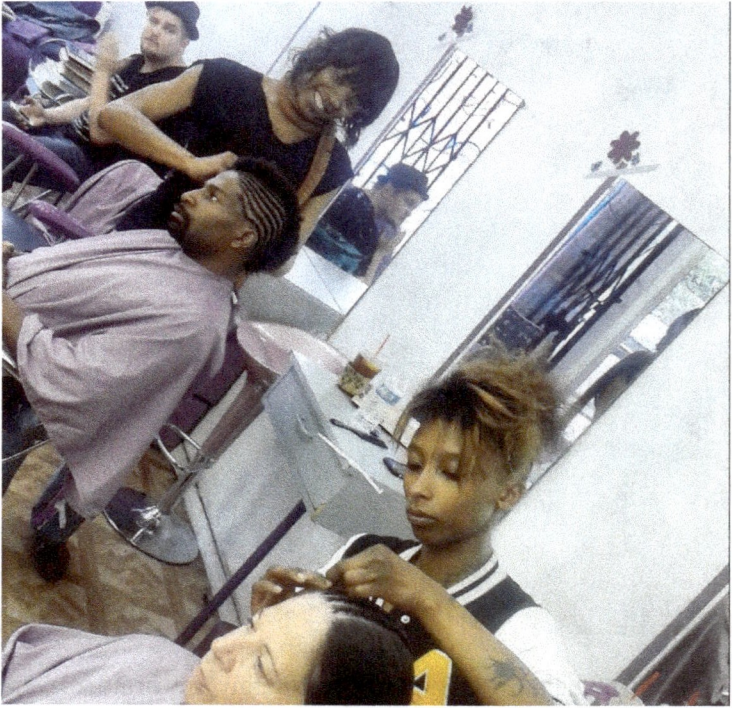

LaPorche and Colleta

8

Consistency Is the Currency of Success

Success is not built in giant leaps, it's built in small, repeated steps done with discipline and intention. Consistency is the currency every entrepreneur must learn to invest. You can have a brilliant idea, a good product, and natural talent, but without consistency, it all crumbles.

The truth is this: **Your business will only be as steady as you are.** Whether you're braiding hair, selling candles, coaching clients, or running a restaurant, consistency is the invisible force that holds your entire business together. It builds trust, attracts customers, and keeps the doors open when others quit.

After 30+ years in the salon industry, here are the foundational habits that helped me grow from a struggling young mother braiding hair out of my house... to running one of the most recognized braid studios in Los Angeles. These steps will help you build a business that is profitable, professional, and unstoppable.

1. Use Timers to Stay Consistent With Advertising

If you're not promoting, you're not growing. Too many entrepreneurs advertise only when business slows down. That's
backwards. Advertising is not a reaction - it's a ritual.

Set **daily or weekly timers** on your phone reminding you to
market your business:
    Post on social media
    Hand out flyers
    Update your business page
    Send follow-up messages
    Reach out to old clients
    Check your Google Business listing
    Marketing must become as routine as brushing your teeth.
Consistency makes your business look alive, active, and worth
trusting.

2. Visualize Your Business — Even Before It Exists

All creation begins in the mind.
    Before I opened my first salon, I saw it clearly in my imagina-
tion, the chairs, the smell of the products, the line of clients at
the door. Spend **five minutes a day** visualizing:

Imagine: The way your business will look
    The customers walking in
    The money flowing with ease
    The joy you feel serving people
    The abundance surrounding your life

Visualization is not fantasy, it's rehearsal.

And when the universe sees you rehearsing, it starts arranging.

3. Write Everything Down — Organization Is Power

A cluttered mind creates a cluttered business.

Get a folder, notebook, binder, planner - anything that keeps your ideas **in one place**.

Write down:

Business goals

Pricing

Appointment policies

Monthly expenses

Supplies needed

New ideas

To-do lists

Future dreams

What gets written down gets done.

Organization is your silent business partner.

4. Build an Email List — Every Entrepreneur Needs One

Never rely solely on social media. Platforms change. Algorithms shift. Accounts get hacked.

Your email list is **your digital real estate**. Have every client sign in, leave name, number, and email.

Use that list to:

Announce promotions

Share updates

Offer discounts
Fill slow days
Stay connected
An email list is one of the smartest, most profitable tools you can own.

5. Be Kinder Than You Have Ever Been

Kindness is a business strategy.

A smile, a compliment, a handshake, these small acts create loyalty that money cannot buy. When a client feels seen, valued, and respected, they return. They refer. They brag about you. The energy you give is the energy your business will attract. Kindness also heals you.

As I grew spiritually, I learned that the energy I put into my business was shaping the women who worked with me. I wasn't just braiding hair, I was creating an environment. I was teaching. I was planting seeds. Be the kind of leader people feel safe with. Be the business owner you wish you had met when you were younger.

6. Never Abandon Direct Marketing

Even in the digital age, **old-school marketing still works**.
   I built my empire with:
Flyers
Posters
Pole signs
Street promotion
Hand-to-hand advertising
And guess what? After 5, 10, 20 years, I still did it.

And it still worked.
Go to:
Local events
Parks
Flea markets
Festivals
Shopping centers

A flyer in someone's hand is still one of the strongest forms of marketing. Stay visible. Stay present. Stay consistent.

7. Master Free Online Marketing

The internet has leveled the playing field.
FREE tools can grow your business if you use them consistently:
Facebook groups
Instagram reels
TikTok videos
Google Business
YouTube
Local hashtags
Community pages
Short motivational messages
Before-and-after photos
Pick one or two platforms and show up regularly.
Not perfectly, but consistently.
The more your name appears, the more your business becomes a brand.

Success Doesn't Respond to Wishes — It Responds to Work

Consistency is not glamorous. It's not the exciting part. It's the quiet, disciplined work behind the scenes. But it is the most powerful business tool you will ever have. When you show up, day after day, even when you're tired... Even when you're scared... Even when you feel like nothing is working... The universe will reward your persistence. Your business will grow. Your confidence will grow. Your income will grow.

Consistency is your magic.

Consistency is your foundation and if you want a sustainable, successful business you must be consistent. Consistency is your currency of success.

Braids By SaBrina Staff working hard

SaBrina teaching a Braiding Class

Audrey, SaBrina, Terica, Barbara

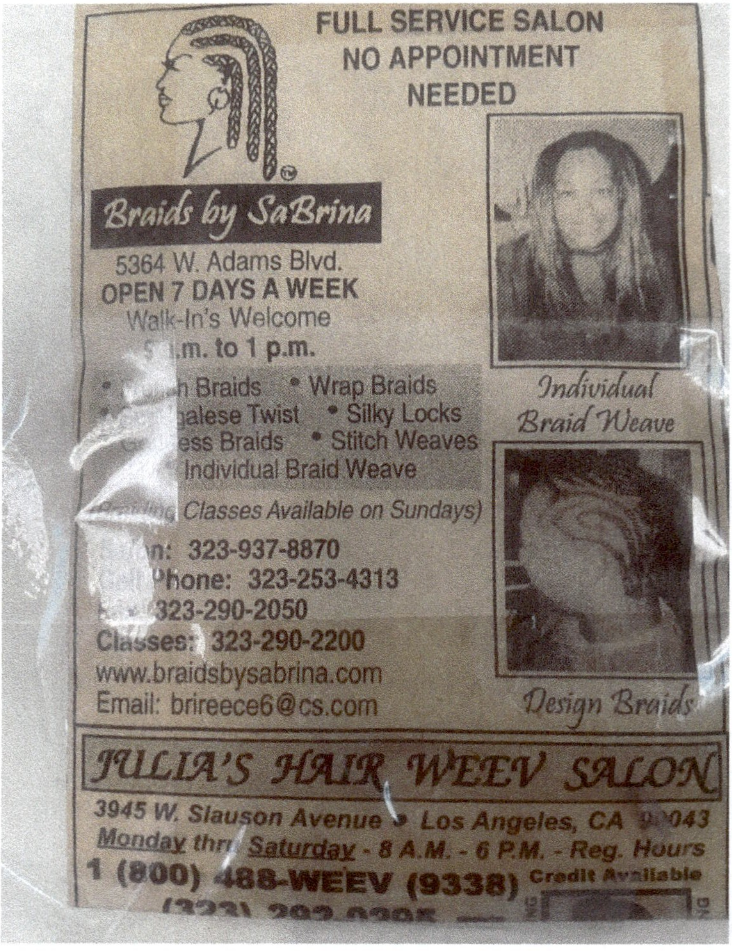

Advertisement in the Los Angeles Sentinel News Paper

Braids By SaBrina Staff when we all wore purple

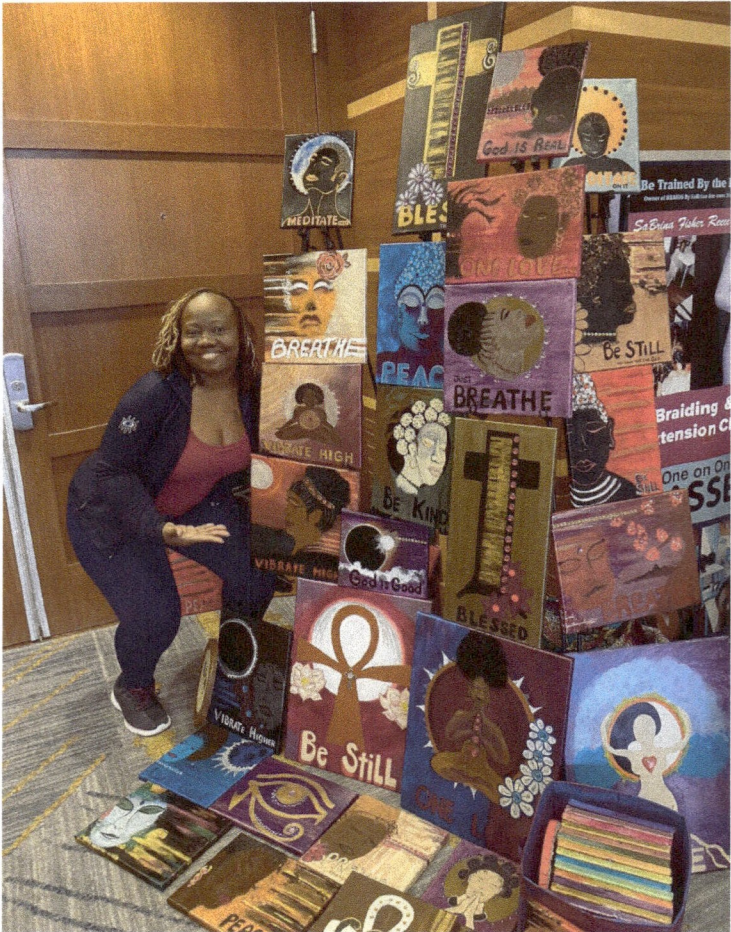

SaBrina Fisher Reece and her "Spiritual Art From My Heart" Collection

9

Pricing & Profit: Getting Paid What You're Worth

If there's one thing I wish someone had taught me at twenty years old, it's this: **A business can survive mistakes in marketing, mistakes in staffing, mistakes in scheduling, but it cannot survive mistakes in pricing.** Your price is the engine of your business. Your profit is the oxygen. Without both, your dream cannot breathe.

Most new entrepreneurs underprice themselves because:
- they want to attract customers
- they are afraid of rejection
- they are comparing themselves to competitors
- they don't feel "qualified enough"
- they don't know their numbers
- they just want people to like them

When I first began braiding at my home in Compton, I was still in the 12th grade, charging just $40. One day, I made the mistake of telling my cousin Ronald Fisher that I'd braid his girlfriend's hair and he could "pay me whatever." Big mistake. I worked for hours, pouring my skills and energy into her hair, and when I finished, he proudly handed me **five dollars**. Five.

That was my first business lesson, and it was priceless:

Never let anyone else decide your worth. Quote your price loud, clear, and unapologetically.

Here's the truth: If you undercharge, you will end up over-worked, undervalued, and resentful. Yes, I've given discounts before, but those were **my decisions**, not because a client pushed for one. That's what real leadership looks like. **You run the business. The business does not run you.**

If you underprice, you sabotage your own success. If you don't understand profit, you'll stay stuck in survival mode instead of stepping into your power. Your price is not just a number — it's a reflection of your confidence, your skill, your experience, and the standard you set for your life. Set it with authority. Stand on it with pride. That's how you build a business, not a burden.

This chapter is designed to keep that from happening to you.

1. Price With Confidence — Not Fear

Your price should reflect:

- your skill
- your time
- your labor
- your experience
- your training

- your overhead
- and your future goals

It should NOT reflect:

- how you feel about yourself that day
- what someone else can or can't afford
- what competitors are charging
- what people think is "reasonable"
- guilt, insecurity, or fear

When you price too low, you are not helping anyone, you're only training people to expect luxury at a discount, once you start low? It's ten times harder to raise your prices later. Set your price based on truth, not timidity.

2. Know Your Numbers or Your Numbers Will Hurt You

Too many entrepreneurs "hope" they are making money instead of **knowing** they are.

Profit is simple math:

PRICE − COST = PROFIT

But you must include ALL costs:

- Rent
- Supplies
- Advertising cost
- Marketing
- Staff
- Gas
- Cleaning supplies

- Insurance
- Credit card fees
- Your time

When you do the math honestly, you may realize you've been undercharging for years. I've seen talented business owners with full schedules, women doing amazing work, barely surviving... because their pricing does not match their workload. Never forget: **A full calendar means nothing if your not making a profit.**

3. Create a Pricing Structure — Not a Guessing Game

Your pricing should be:

- written down
- posted
- consistent
- sent to client before appointment
- clear
- emotionally neutral

When you change your price based on your mood or how busy you are, clients lose trust. When you stand firm, clients feel secure, because consistency is professionalism.

4. Charge for Your Time, Not Just Your Skill

This is the mistake MOST service-based entrepreneurs make.
Yes, people pay for your skill.
But skill is only half of the equation.

People must also pay for:

- your speed
- your efficiency
- your expertise
- your preparation
- your years of practice
- your correction of their mistakes
- the comfortable environment you create
- the entertainment while being serviced
- your ability to fix what others ruin

If it takes you 8 hours, that is 8 hours away from your:

- children
- rest
- spouse
- creativity
- business growth
- self-care

Your time is valuable. Period! Don't be arrogant about it but be firm.

5. Stop Feeling Guilty for Charging Properly

Let me free you right now:
   Your business is not a charity.
   You are not responsible for anyone else's financial situation.
   Discounts are optional, not required.
   You can be kind AND still get paid fully.

You can be compassionate AND maintain your pricing. You can help people AND still protect your livelihood. Discounts should be:

- strategic
- occasional
- never pressured
- never begged for
- and NEVER expected

Generosity is beautiful. Being taken advantage of is not.

6. Raise Your Prices as Your Skill Increases

As your business grows, your prices must grow with you. I raise my prices every January 1st by $20 to $100.

Raise your prices when:

- you get more skilled
- you get faster
- you get more clients
- your demand increases
- your overhead increases
- your quality improves

If you don't raise your prices, you will feel resentment and resentment kills creativity. Raising your price is not greed, it is alignment. It's the natural flow of any business.

7. Don't Let Clients Negotiate Your Worth

People negotiate cars, houses, furniture, but they should NOT negotiate your talent.

Why? Because negotiation implies:

- you don't know your worth
- your price is flexible
- they can control the interaction

Your answer must always be:

"Unfortunately, my prices are firm."

However: You don't owe an explanation. You don't owe a justification. You don't owe a discount. Your price is your boundary.

I would post a sign that says "Prices Increase Yearly"

8. Profit Is Not What You Make - It's What You Keep

When the money comes in, don't get excited. Instead make sure you get organized.

You need to has:

- savings
- taxes set aside
- emergency fund
- marketing budget
- reinvestment plan

Many businesses collapse not from lack of clients...but from lack of planning.

You must treat your profit like a seed, not a meal.
Some of your profit must be planted.
Some must be protected.
Some must be reinvested.
Some must be saved.
Some must be enjoyed.
But ALL of it must be respected.

Price with courage knowing that you have perfected the skill that you offer. Operate with structure and pride. Know your numbers and don't flip back and forth with the prices. Protect your profit. Stand on your worth. Price your service and stick to it. I personally make customers aware that prices increase every January 1st. Then you will receive less push back. They know ahead of time and you feel you are able to fairly increase your price in a systematic and structured way.

You did not come this far to run a business that drains you. You came to create a business that:

- supports you
- frees you
- liberates you
- elevates you
- blesses your family
- and leaves a legacy

Pricing is not just money - it is self-respect in numerical form.
Once you master pricing and profit, your business will finally have the foundation it needs to grow, thrive, and sustain you for years to come.

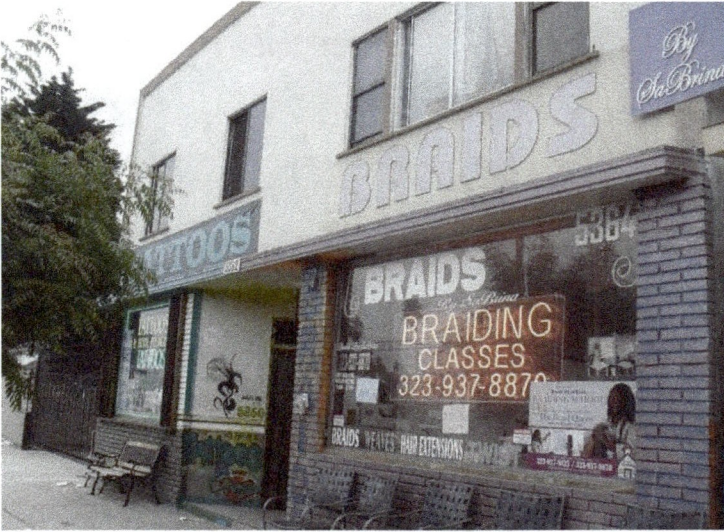

My Tattoo shop was next door to my Braiding Shop. I used to call it 'SaBrina Avenue"

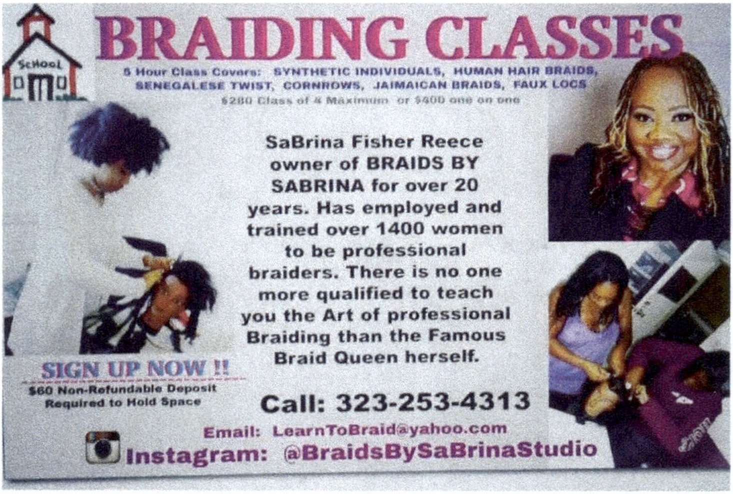

Braiding Class Flyer

My Braider Barbara doing my son Justin's hair

SaBrina testifying in Sacramento about the Braiding Licensing

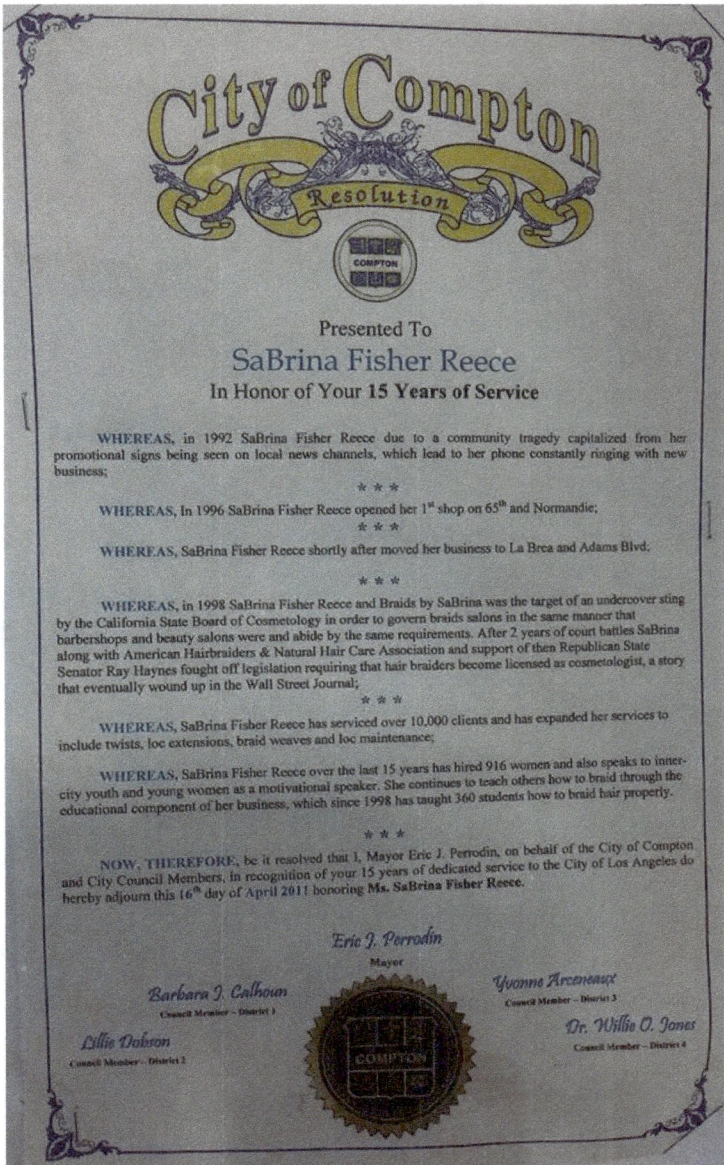

City of Compton

Resolution

COMPTON

Presented To

SaBrina Fisher Reece

In Honor of Your **15 Years of Service**

WHEREAS, in 1992 SaBrina Fisher Reece due to a community tragedy capitalized from her promotional signs being seen on local news channels, which lead to her phone constantly ringing with new business;

* * *

WHEREAS, In 1996 SaBrina Fisher Reece opened her 1st shop on 65th and Normandie;

* * *

WHEREAS, SaBrina Fisher Reece shortly after moved her business to La Brea and Adams Blvd.

* * *

WHEREAS, in 1998 SaBrina Fisher Reece and Braids by SaBrina was the target of an undercover sting by the California State Board of Cosmetology in order to govern braids salons in the same manner that barbershops and beauty salons were and abide by the same requirements. After 2 years of court battles SaBrina along with American Hairbraiders & Natural Hair Care Association and support of then Republican State Senator Ray Haynes fought off legislation requiring that hair braiders become licensed as cosmetologist, a story that eventually wound up in the Wall Street Journal;

* * *

WHEREAS, SaBrina Fisher Reece has serviced over 10,000 clients and has expanded her services to include twists, loc extensions, braid weaves and loc maintenance;

WHEREAS, SaBrina Fisher Reece over the last 15 years has hired 916 women and also speaks to inner-city youth and young women as a motivational speaker. She continues to teach others how to braid through the educational component of her business, which since 1998 has taught 360 students how to braid hair properly.

* * *

NOW, THEREFORE, be it resolved that I, Mayor Eric J. Perrodin, on behalf of the City of Compton and City Council Members, in recognition of your 15 years of dedicated service to the City of Los Angeles do hereby adjourn this 16th day of April 2011 honoring **Ms. SaBrina Fisher Reece**.

Eric J. Perrodin
Mayor

Barbara J. Calhoun
Council Member – District 1

Yvonne Arceneaux
Council Member – District 3

Lillie Dobson
Council Member – District 2

Dr. Willie O. Jones
Council Member – District 4

COMPTON

www.In59SecondsPublishing.com

May 22, 2014 · 🌐

Just In case you Missed it...Torrei Hart ex wife of Kevin Hart appeared on the View with my Beautiful Sisterlock Extensions in her hair. Yes I did her Hair.....she is such a nice woman...She makes my work look fabulous. .tune into her new Reality show coming... See more

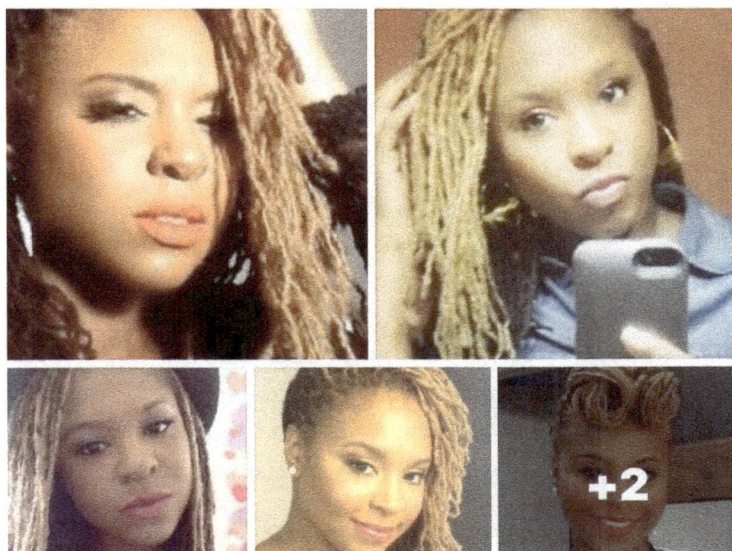

When I created beautiful Loc Extensions on Torrei Hart (Kevin Hart's ex–wife)

10

The Heart Behind the Hustle

A Legacy of Love, Leadership & Healing

When people talk about entrepreneurship, they often focus on numbers, strategy, and marketing. But my journey, the true story behind *Braids By SaBrina,* was never about that. My story was about **people**. About **healing**. About **not becoming a statistic**. About **survival**. About **sisterhood**. About the sacredness of community.

It was about the hearts and hands of Black women who walked through my doors and changed my life as much as I changed theirs. I had the privilege of teaching young women a skill that would help them support themselves and their families.

I did not build my business alone. God gave me a vision at a young age, with no formal education and no specific business skill other than knowing how to braid hair. I built it with the spirits of more than **1,700 braiders** who stepped into my salon over 30 years, young women, mothers, college students, dreamers, survivors, women who were powerful even when they didn't know it yet. Many came to me broken, hopeful, lost, determined, or quietly carrying the same childhood wounds I was still healing within myself.

And through the grace of God... **we healed together.**

Growing Up While Guiding Others

When I opened my first salon, I was twenty-six. Young. Hurt. Angry. A survivor of abandonment and trauma. I didn't know healing was possible. All I was ever told was, *"Just go pray about it."* And at that time, I felt abandoned by God.

I lost my beloved grandmother, the only mother I truly had. She raised me and my sister Mary because both our parents were addicts. She took us in when Mary was a year old and I was three months old, after my drug-ridden mother put me into a suitcase and tried to take my life.

So I began my journey with **fierce determination,** determined to prove I deserved to be here. Determined to survive. Determined to rise. I was hardworking and fierce... but far from healed. When you grow up in dysfunction, you lead with tension in your shoulders and fire in your voice. I demanded excellence because I didn't yet know how to ask for it gently.

But even then, **I loved those girls.** I cared for them long before I had the emotional vocabulary to express it. As I transformed spiritually, I became calmer, wiser, softer, they were right beside me. My staff didn't just witness my evolution...They were part of it.

They saw the rough version of me, the transitioning version of me, and the blossoming version of me. They watched me grow into the healed woman I am today.

The Blind Leading the Blind - A Hard Leadership Lesson

I will never forget one of the wildest moments of my life, the day I learned how deeply I needed to grow as a leader.

I was dating a man named Percy. A fresh divorce behind me, a six-year-old son, and an infant daughter. I threw Justin a birthday party and invited Percy. He said he would come... but he didn't and triggered something inside me. I felt rejected.

In my hurt, I made a terrible decision: I convinced **five** of my staff members to ride with me to his barbershop and beat him up. OMG. Yep! Beat him up. lol Not ONE of them said, "Bri... this is a bad idea."

The blind leading the blind. We pulled up. I called him outside. They surrounded him exactly as I had instructed them to do. My plan was to swing first so they would follow. Hitting him from the right, left and back. But when the moment came... **I chickened out.** I couldn't bring myself to swing.

Percy, being ex-military, instantly recognized what was happening. In one swift motion, he swept both himself and me out of the circle, using some kind of military tactic that left everyone stunned. And then he lectured me. He told me how much danger I put myself and my braiders in. He told me he carried a gun and could have shot all of us. He walked me inside and showed me the gun, not to threaten me, but to show me the seriousness of my actions.

I was dead wrong. We all laughed about it years later, but that moment changed me.

It was the moment I realized: I had a responsibility to lead correctly. To protect, not endanger. To guide, not react. To grow up for the sake of the women who trusted me.

That was three decades ago. My son is now 36. I had no sense back then, but that moment became **pivotal** in shaping me as a woman and as a leader. I learned that I had a responsibility to lead correctly and wisely. These young women were looking up to me and I could never lead them into chaos again.

The Salon Was a Sanctuary

A salon is not just a place to get your hair done.
   A salon is:

- a sanctuary
- a classroom
- a healing circle
- a safe space for people to vent
- a breathing space
- a confidence builder

I taught my staff much more than braiding.
   I taught them:

- how to save money
- how to open mutual funds
- how to stay consistent
- how to problem solve
- how to speak kindly, even when annoyed
- how to run their own businesses

But in return, they taught me:

- patience
- compassion
- loyalty
- softness
- reflection
- how to control emotions
- how to see myself through others' eyes

We were mirrors for each other. In helping them find their footing, I found mine.

From Boss to Mentor to Mama-SaBrina

At first, I was "the tiny boss with the big energy."
But over time, I became:

- a mentor
- a motivator
- a spiritual guide
- a mother figure
- a voice of direction when life was loud

When I began motivational speaking, I invited the Braiders to listen. They didn't have to, but they did. They encouraged me and supported me. They allowed me to grow in front of them.

I used to call them my "guinea pigs." But truthfully, I was honored. They trusted me even when I was still learning myself. They were helping me become the woman I am today. Those years were sacred, every conversation, every laugh, every staff outing, every shared moment of sisterhood.

Messages That Still Touch My Soul

I have received many texts, dm's , emails and phone calls from my Past Braiders. Telling me how much they loved and appreciated me. Many even took the time to apologize, but i hold no grudges. I forgive them and pray they forgive me as well. We were learning and growing together. These are just a few:

From Lashanna:

My Wonderful Belizean, salon manager of ten beautiful years. She's a good person:

"Today is such a special day – a day to celebrate you, Bri,
the incredible woman
who has brought so much love, wisdom, and joy into so
many lives, including mine.
56 years of grace, strength, and beautiful memories, and
yet you continue to
shine brighter with each passing year.
You've been a guiding light – a sister, a friend, and a
blessing to everyone who knows you.
Your kindness, laughter, and unwavering faith inspire us
all.
Whether through your warm hugs, your wise words, or
your generous heart, you make the world a better place
just by being in it.
On your birthday, I pray God fills your day with love,
peace, and all the

happiness you deserve.
May this year bring you good health, sweet moments,
and countless reasons to smile.
You are cherished more than you will ever know.
Happy 56th birthday, Bri.
Here's to many more wonderful years ahead.
With all my love,
Lashanna & Family."

From Shavon:

Shavon was a natural hustler like me. She is also one I grew to love dearly. She didn't always see her beauty or recognize her greatness but she was a good person and a very talented braider.

Bri, I apreciate your voice and you as the uniquely made woman you are and have become. you played a major role in my life and I see you keep up the scholar work. You motivate me than and now. I really appreciate you SaBrina you are a blessing.
-Shavon wright

From Terica (China Tight Eyes):

A talented braider who worked for me for eight years, I grew to love her as family:

"Hey Miss Beautiful,
I'm just looking at your Instagram this morning with a smile on my face. You are still so beautiful.

I was thinking about you, I actually saw your sister yesterday.
I was thinking about you, SaBrina, and I just wanted to say thank you, thank you from the bottom of my heart.
The love that you showed me is just amazing, and I think about it all the time.
I talk about you all the time.
I learned from you, and I still would love to learn more from you because as a woman who has been through it and has grown and knows my place, my value, and my worth...
Yes, I want to say thank you, Bri, for always showing a Black woman that she was valuable, that she had self-esteem, that she could be successful individually.
You never let anything stop you, and you always motivated me and others to do better.
Regardless of what I was going through, you never judged me and you always loved me for who I was.
And I just really wanted to say this from the bottom of my heart:
I love you, and thank you."
-Terica

From Melanie:

She and I had our challenges but I loved her and wanted so much for her, more than she wanted for herself at times. Inside she was a good person who just couldn't always see it.

"Bri, I love you, you are the only boss that keeps it real with me. I wish you would braid my hair one day because you are the Queen of braids and I crown myself the princess. I will never forget what you taught me Bri. Thank you so much"
-Melanie

From LaPorche :

One of the sweetest spirits I have ever known, she worked for me over 6 years.

"I want to give you flowers SaBrina for all that you have done for me and others.
You expressed your love and care to me as a mother. I met you when I was younger in my early twenties. You gave me an amazing opportunity to work at you salon. I did not know I was going to be gifted with more. You taught me more than braiding. You taught me basics to higher levels of consciousness. When I first met you I was going through a lot. I was going through depression. You cared for me as your own child. SaBrina, you introduced me to better things in life/ a better way to live this life time. I can go on and on and on about how you have helped me in so many ways. I will always remember you beautiful pure-hearted soul.
A breath of fresh air is what I felt when I met you Bri. All of your

accomplishments
has been an inspiration to me. I am truly thankful for your
amazing soul.
Thank you SaBrina for U
-LaPorche

I was humbled and brought to tears rereading these messages. There are so many more, lost in old phones, old emails, old memories, but each one reminds me that they did not have to say those kind words but they did and I will love them all forever.

The Blessing of Being Able to Give

Sometimes I look back and marvel at how a little Black girl from Compton - abandoned, traumatized, raising herself through pain, grew up to employ nearly two thousand women. Giving them the security:

To pay their rent.
To help feed their children.
To teach them a trade.
To remind them of their value.
To give them second chances.
To talk to them about God, vibration, discipline, and love.
To show them possibilities beyond what they could see.
To teach then that "All Things are Possible" no matter where you came from.

I'm forever grateful to have been able to teach them but that was not just me. That was **God** moving through me. I was always positive, but I wasn't always healed. Yet God trusted me with His daughters anyway.

The Legacy I Leave Behind

Some measure success by money. Some by awards. Some by possessions. I measure mine by:

- the women who return after 5, 10, 20 years
- the laughter we shared
- the healing we experienced
- the kindness we created
- the dreams they fulfilled
- the hearts we touched

That is my legacy.

If entrepreneurship taught me anything, it's this:

Entrepreneurship is not about money. It's about people.

It's about lifting others while you climb.

It's about offering grace because someone once offered you grace.

It's about evolving - from hurt to healed, from strict to supportive, from boss to leader.

My greatest accomplishment was not just building a successful salon.

My greatest accomplishment was not just building Braids By SaBrina it was building women, building positive relationships. Helping them see their beauty.

Helping them discover their strength. Helping them realize their future was bigger than their past.

To every braider, every young woman, every sister who walked into my salon:

I Love You, Thank you.

Thank you for trusting me.

Thank you for learning with me.

Thank you for forgiving me during the seasons when I was still learning myself.

Thank you for letting me grow into the woman I am today.

You were not just part of my business - you were part of my history and my healing

And that will forever be one of the greatest blessings of my entire life.

Marla and SaBrina 1997

Braiding School

138

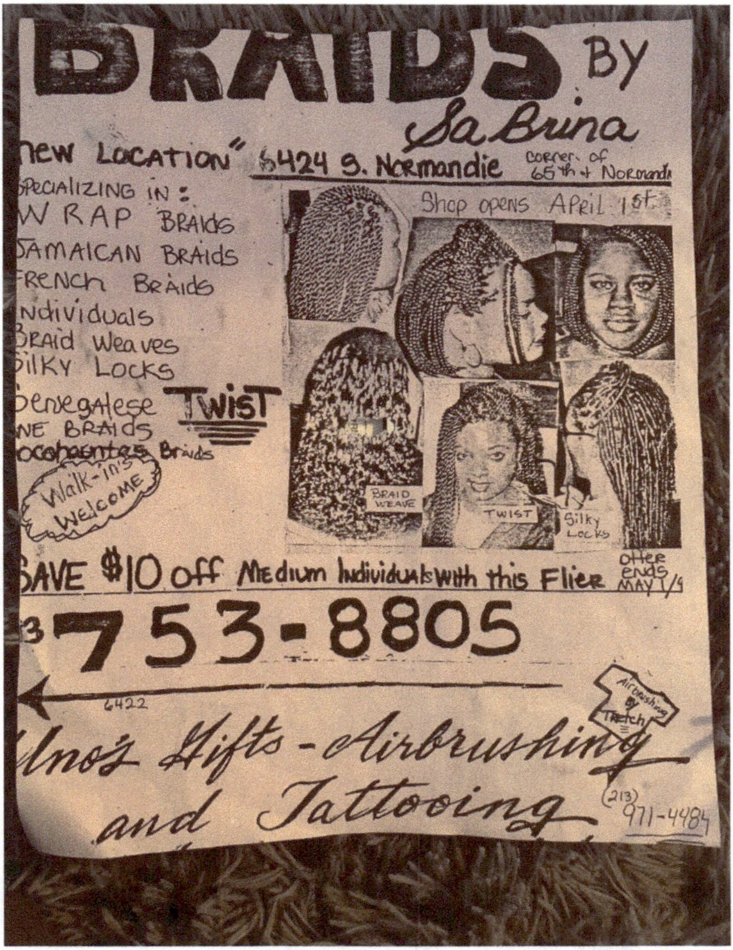

One of Braids By SaBrina very first flyers

The Braids By SaBrina Staff at the 15th Anniversary

140

Braids by SaBrina Summer 2011 Staff
323-937-8825

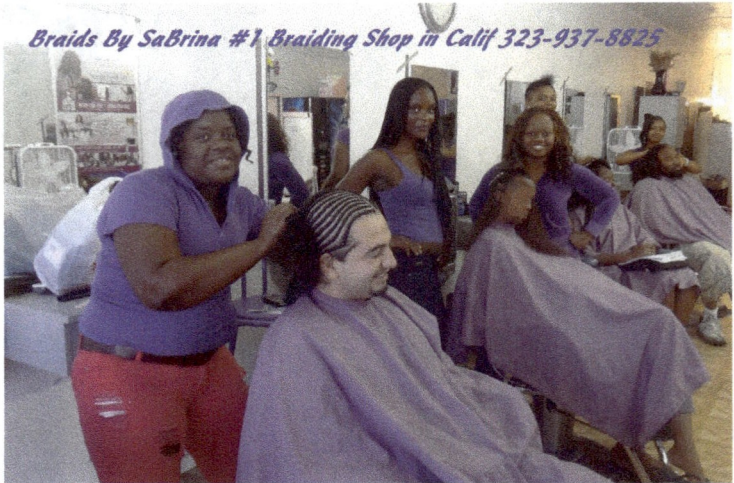

Braids By SaBrina #1 Braiding Shop in Calif 323-937-8825

About the Author

SaBrina Fisher Reece is a powerhouse entrepreneur, author, and visionary leader who has spent more than three decades building successful businesses from the ground up. Known for her bold work ethic, her intuitive leadership style, and her ability to turn challenges into opportunities, SaBrina opened her first business at just twenty-six years old and never looked back.

She is the founder of several well-known brands, including **Braids By SaBrina**, **A New Vision Dreadlock Studio**, **Just-In Time Barber Shop**, and **Inked 4 Life Tattoo Studio** - each one created through discipline, passion, and an unwavering commitment to excellence. Through these companies, SaBrina has employed and mentored thousands of people, offering not just jobs, but stability, opportunity, and guidance to those who trusted her leadership.

Beyond entrepreneurship, SaBrina is a multi-book author

whose work inspires, empowers, and speaks directly to the heart. Her titles include:

My Spiritual Smile, **Kicking Depression in the Butt**, **Become Your own Cheerleader**, **Your Mind Is Magic**, **How to Make More Money in 2026**, **Family Fun Night Cookbook**, **When I Say "I AM"**, **Sexuality & Spirituality**, **Living Life on a Higher Frequency and Perfectly Positive** books that reflect her personal growth, spiritual evolution, and deep belief in in self - transformation.

In **Small Business Basics**, SaBrina brings her raw honesty, real-life experience, and spiritual wisdom to the world of entrepreneurship. She writes not from theory but from decades of hands-on leadership, hiring, training, building teams, creating systems, and navigating the highs and lows of running multiple businesses simultaneously. Her lessons come from lived experience, earned hard work, and divine guidance.

Today, SaBrina continues to inspire others through her writing, speaking, and mentorship, reminding people everywhere that success is possible when you lead with vision, discipline, faith, and heart. She is living proof that you can build a thriving business and a beautiful life - one decision, one belief, and one brave step at a time.

You can connect with me on:

f https://www.facebook.com/BraidQueenSaBrinaReece

Also by SaBrina Fisher Reece

SaBrina Fisher Reece's body of work spans personal develop-
ment, spirituality, emotional wellness, and entrepreneurship.
Her books provide clear guidance on mindset mastery, faith-
based manifestation, positive identity, effective prayer, emotional balance, sexual-spiritual harmony, and the fundamen-
tals of building and sustaining a small business. Together, her
titles offer a comprehensive blueprint for improving both inner
life and external success—making her an author dedicated
to empowering readers on every level: spiritual, emotional,
mental, and practical.

Sexuality & Spirituality

Sexuality & Spirituality invites you to look
deeper into the heart, the body, and the
soul. It is a gentle yet powerful reminder
that intimacy is more than physical - it is
energetic, emotional, and deeply spiritual.
This book helps you understand your patterns, heal old wounds, and open yourself to
connections rooted in truth, wholeness, and divine alignment.

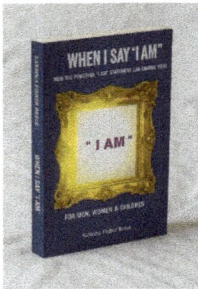

When I Say "I AM"

What you say after "I Am" has the power to shape your entire life.

In *When I Say "I Am"*, SaBrina Fisher Reece reveals the sacred and scientific power of spoken identity. Blending spiritual truth, biblical wisdom, and universal law, this transformational book teaches readers how their words are not just communication—but creation. Every "I Am" statement becomes a command to the subconscious, a signal to the universe, and a declaration to the spiritual realm.

Drawing from scripture, including God's revelation of "I AM" as the eternal source of being, SaBrina shows how the same creative force lives within each of us. Through emotionally moving insight, practical affirmations, and deep spiritual awareness, readers learn how to shift from fear-based language to faith-based declarations that activate healing, confidence, abundance, and purpose.

This book will help you:

Break negative identity patterns

Reprogram limiting beliefs

Speak life instead of fear

Align your words with divine promise

Use "I Am" as a daily tool for transformation

More than motivation, *When I Say "I Am"* is a blueprint for conscious creation. It reminds you that your voice is powerful, your identity is sacred, and your words are always working— either for you or against you.

If you are ready to stop speaking survival and start speaking destiny, this book will show you how to command your life with intention, faith, and divine authority—one "I Am" at a time.

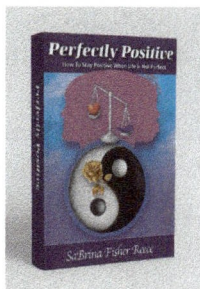

Perfectly Positive: How to Stay positive when Life is Not Perfect

Perfectly Positive is your guide to staying centered, grounded, and hopeful in an imperfect world. Through real-life stories, practical tools, and soul-level wisdom, SaBrina Fisher Reece shows you how to rise above daily stress, disappointments, and negative thinking to create a life rooted in peace and purpose. This book teaches you how to master your thoughts, elevate your vibration, and choose a positive perspective—even when life isn't cooperating. Inspiring, relatable, and deeply transformative, *Perfectly Positive* reminds you that happiness is not found in perfection... it's created by the power of your own mi

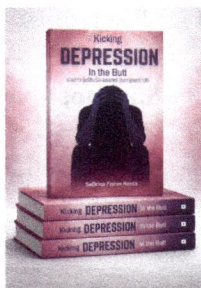

Kicking Depression in the Butt

Kicking Depression in the Butt is a raw, faith-infused, and deeply practical guide for anyone who is tired of surviving in silence and ready to reclaim their life.

Drawing from her own lived experiences with trauma, abandonment, loss, and depression, SaBrina Fisher Reece invites readers into an honest conversation about what depression really feels like, and how to fight back. This book does not minimize pain or offer shallow positivity. Instead, it helps readers recognize depression as an internal enemy, interrupt destructive thought cycles, and rebuild their inner world with intention, truth, and daily tools that actually work.

Through personal storytelling, spiritual insight, and mindset-shifting strategies, SaBrina shows readers how to stop identifying with their darkest thoughts and begin designing a life that protects their peace. She addresses the realities of trauma, triggers, boundaries, faith, therapy, medication, and personal responsibility, offering a balanced approach that honors both professional support and inner work.

Kicking Depression in the Butt is for the person who keeps showing up while quietly falling apart. It is for those who smile while suffering, who feel strong on the outside but exhausted on the inside. Most of all, it is a reminder that depression may visit, but it does not get to stay, and it does not get to become your identity.

This book is not about perfection. It's about progress. It's about learning how to fight for your mind, your peace, and your future, one thought, one choice, and one day at a time.

Because as long as you have breath in your body, your story

is not over—and you still have the power to kick depression in the butt.

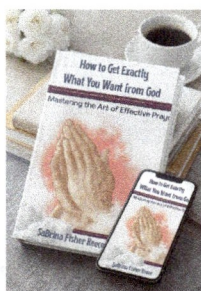

How to Get Exactly What You Want From God

How to Get Exactly What You Want From God shows you how to pray with results. Inside, you'll learn how to make specific requests, build the faith needed to sustain them, and match your thoughts and emotions to the outcome you want. SaBrina teaches you how to interrupt negative self-talk, eliminate doubt, and step into a mindset that attracts divine answers quickly and clearly. This is your guide to intentional prayer, spiritual alignment, and receiving blessings without hesitation.

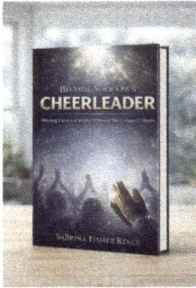

Become Your Own Cheerleader

Become Your Own Cheerleader: Moving Forward in Life Without the Support of Others is a powerful, honest guide for anyone who has ever felt unseen, unsupported, or overlooked by the very people they hoped would cheer the loudest.

In this deeply personal and transformational book, SaBrina Fisher Reece invites readers into her life story, one shaped by early abandonment, profound loss, resilience, and hard-earned self-trust. From surviving childhood trauma and the murder of the grandmother who raised her, to building businesses, writing books, and leading without consistent support, SaBrina reveals what happens when you stop waiting for applause and start standing firmly in your own worth.

This is not a book about bitterness. It is a book about liberation.

Through raw storytelling and hard truths, you will learn why some people cannot clap for you, how to stop taking silence personally, and why your worth is never up for a vote. You will discover how to release the need for validation, acknowledge the few who truly support you, and become the voice you once needed to hear from others.

Each chapter builds toward one essential truth: the most powerful support you will ever receive must come from within.

Whether you are navigating family disappointment, friendship distance, professional invisibility, or emotional independence, **Become Your Own Cheerleader** offers clarity, comfort, and courage. It teaches you how to keep going when no one is watching, how to celebrate yourself without guilt, and how to live boldly without waiting for permission.

This book is for the strong ones who got strong too early. For the ones who kept showing up. For the ones who learned how to clap for themselves.

If you are ready to stop waiting for approval and start living like you believe in you, this book is for you.

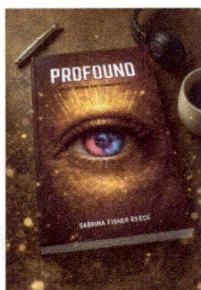

Profound 4 Book Series
Introduction to the Profound Series

This series was not written to convince you of anything.

It was written to remind you of something.

For most of my life, I searched for answers the same way many people do. I looked outward. I prayed, studied, worked, endured, and tried to become better by force. I believed growth meant effort alone and that transformation required suffering. I was taught, as many of us are, what to believe, what to question, and what to avoid.

What I did not realize at the time was that I was not missing faith.

I was missing understanding.

The *Profound Series* was born from a deeply personal journey of self-discovery, healing, and expansion. It is the result of decades of reading ancient texts, studying metaphysical teachings, reflecting on spiritual principles, and most importantly, applying this wisdom in real life. This series is not meant to replace religion, tradition, or belief systems. It is meant to widen the lens.

Religion offers structure, community, and devotion. Ancient wisdom offers context, depth, and responsibility. Together, they reveal something powerful: that you are not separate from the divine, and you were never meant to live disconnected from your inner power.

This series exists because I discovered that much of what we are seeking has already been known for centuries. Long before modern psychology, neuroscience, or self-help, ancient philosophers, mystics, teachers, and spiritual scholars understood the relationship between thought, emotion, consciousness, and reality. They understood that the mind is creative, that belief shapes experience, and that life responds to awareness.

The first book, **Profound**, is about remembering. It is about gathering ancient wisdom and recognizing truths that may feel familiar even if you are encountering them for the first time. This is the awakening stage. The moment when something inside you says, "There is more."

The second book, **Activate**, is about embodiment. Knowledge alone does not change a life. It must be practiced. This book moves wisdom from the intellect into daily living. It teaches you how to tap into the divine energy within you and apply what you have learned in practical, grounded ways.

The third book, **Think**, is about mastery of the mind. Thought is not passive. It is creative. This book guides you in becoming aware of your inner dialogue, understanding how thoughts shape experience, and learning how to consciously direct the mental patterns that influence your life.

The fourth book, **Live**, is about integration. This is where knowledge, practice, and awareness become who you are. You no longer strive to be aligned. You live aligned. You move through the world with clarity, compassion, and confidence, embodying the wisdom you have gained.

Together, these four books form a complete journey.

Awakening. Activation. Mastery. Expression.

This is not a quick fix. It is not spiritual bypassing. It is not about perfection. It is about responsibility. Responsibility for your thoughts. Responsibility for your emotional state. Responsibility for the energy you bring into the world.

The world does not need more information. It needs more conscious people. People who are self-aware. People who understand cause and effect at the level of thought and emotion. People who can pause, reflect, and respond instead of react. People who live from inner alignment rather than fear.

You were never meant to live small, disconnected, or powerless. You were meant to participate in your own evolution.

This series is an invitation. Not to abandon what you believe, but to expand it. Not to follow me, but to follow your own inner knowing. Not to search endlessly outside yourself, but to reconnect with what has always been within you.

If you are reading this, you are ready.

Ready to remember.

Ready to activate.

Ready to master your mind.

Ready to live fully.

Welcome to the journey.

How Do I Control My Emotions?

How Do I Control My Emotions?

When Anger, Rage, and Impulsive Behavior Is Destroying Your Life

Anger does not make you powerful. It makes you reactive. And unchecked reactions can quietly dismantle your relationships, your health, your career, and your peace.

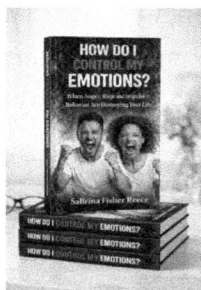

In **How Do I Control My Emotions?**, author and transformational voice **SaBrina Fisher Reece** takes you on a deeply honest journey through emotional self-mastery. Drawing from her own lived experiences as a business owner, leader, and woman who once wore anger as armor, SaBrina exposes the real roots of rage, impulsive behavior, and emotional outbursts, and shows you how to take your power back.

This book is not about suppressing emotions or pretending everything is fine. It is about understanding why you react the way you do, identifying hidden triggers tied to abandonment, trauma, and unmet needs, and learning how to pause, choose, and respond with intention instead of regret.

Inside these pages, you will learn:

Why anger feels justified in the moment but costs you in the long run

How unhealed pain disguises itself as control, dominance, or intensity

The difference between reacting and responding

Why emotional discipline is a form of self-respect

How to stop letting your past control your present

Written with compassion, clarity, and accountability, this book is a call to action for anyone tired of apologizing, repairing damage, or living with the consequences of emotional explosions. If you are ready to stop being ruled by anger and start living from self-control, awareness, and peace, this book will meet you exactly where you are.

You cannot control other people.

But you can always control **you**.

And that changes everything.

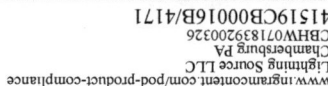